AF247550

RECURRENT
VISIONS

RECURRENT VISIONS

The Architecture of Marshall Brown Projects

Marshall Brown and Karen Kice

———

PRINCETON ARCHITECTURAL PRESS · NEW YORK

Contents

Fig. 1: Foam study model of the Dequindre Civic Academy superimposed upon Roberto Burle Marx's *Garden Design for Beach House for Mr. and Mrs. Burton Tremaine*, project, Santa Barbara, California, 2016. Foam and digital prints.

Foreword

—

Mónica Ponce de León

What arises when we first consider architecture as a cultural, discursive practice that only sometimes—if we are lucky—results in building? For many years, Marshall Brown has engagingly explored the implications of this expansive approach, drawing threads across time to conceive new futures for urban environments and their dwellers. This publication, sparked by his exhibition at the Princeton University School of Architecture in 2019, examines Brown's innovative methods and diverse outputs and emphatically affirms his place as one of the most exciting voices in the discipline today.

Given the contention of increased environmental pressures with contemporary capitalist forces, questions at the scale of the city are all the more pertinent to architecture in our present era. The field of urban design, however, has remained relatively dormant, and there are few practitioners who have made urban issues the focus of their scholarship, research, and creative practice. The discourse has long been dominated by ecological concerns, with an emphasis on the morphology of cities. One area in particular has been persistently understudied: the relationship between ecological issues, economic concerns, and their impact on culture and society. In this context, Brown's work undoubtedly stands out as leading the field. His approach is conceptual yet incisive, displaying a rare sense of intellectual imagination and suggesting prescient alternatives to current realities.

Brown's projects and writings have been widely recognized as some of the few to tackle uneven development and urban decentralization by linking cultural heritage to form, economy, and ecology. The three proposals spotlighted in this volume—The UNITY Plan, Smooth Growth Urbanism®, and the Dequindre Civic Academy—reflect his deep engagement with these endlessly evolving concerns. In each, Brown displays a unique facility for negotiating ambitious, multivalent responses to sociopolitical context, acknowledging individual and collective impulses in pursuit of better relational outcomes for all. In crafting new ideas from old legacies through his use of collage, Brown's dynamic rethinking of the design of cities represents a singular contribution to the discipline.

With his new visions of how to integrate architecture, infrastructure, and landscape, Brown also delves into existing notions regarding what, exactly, ought to be nurtured by a building or a civic space. The choice to respond by constructing potentialities is an assertion of the preeminent need for flexibility; as is manifest in this publication, Brown gestures toward a paradigm shift for the future of urban design as a whole—and I look forward to witnessing the fruition of its nuance.

Millions of pilgrims
Immediately descended upon the City of Chicago
When Oprah Winfrey left this earth on Her 120th birthday.

These hordes of global disciples knew Her simply as The Oprah,
And the institutional complex that She left behind became
A holy city.

She sold the Oprah Winfrey Network in 2015
And returned to Chicago, because California's financial collapse
Made the growth of Her new media empire in Los Angeles
Seem increasingly unlikely.

As fate would have it,
The simultaneous financial crisis in Illinois
Provided the opening She needed
To reestablish Her good works in Chicago.

Mayor Rahm Emanuel's infrastructure development trust
Was a solution to the state and federal budget cuts
That had left Chicago's roads and transit systems crumbling.

Sensing an opportunity, Ms. Winfrey proposed that
In exchange for an unprecedented injection of capital,
She would receive development rights
To certain sites in the Central Area.
Former Mayor Daley, and Mayor Emanuel served as Her brokers
With the Illinois legislature and Obama administration.

By the time the deal was done,
Ms. Winfrey had acquired perpetual leases on air rights
Over Interstate 290, the Circle Interchange,
And the Kennedy Expressway.
No one could have anticipated the great developments that followed.

By the time Oprah Media, known as OM,
Became fully operational in ten short years,
Ms. Winfrey's expanding wealth had driven Her notorious generosity
To even greater heights.

In 2020, She offered to pay off the mortgage debt
Of any property owners in the Central Area,
If they relinquished all rights to any future sales.
Not surprisingly, most of the wealthy declined,
But the vast majority of middle-class businesses
And homeowners willingly accepted,
Since their property values had not increased for fifteen years.

She also built new housing blocks for the poor.
Impeccable management and family development programs,
Insured that most families only lived there for a few years,
Thus eliminating any comparisons to the public housing
That had once plagued Chicago.

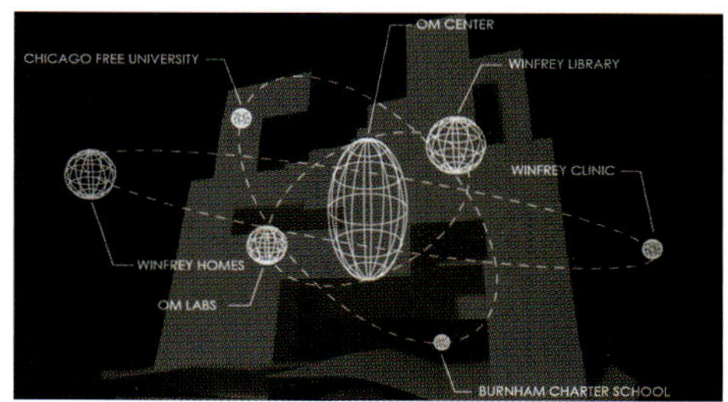

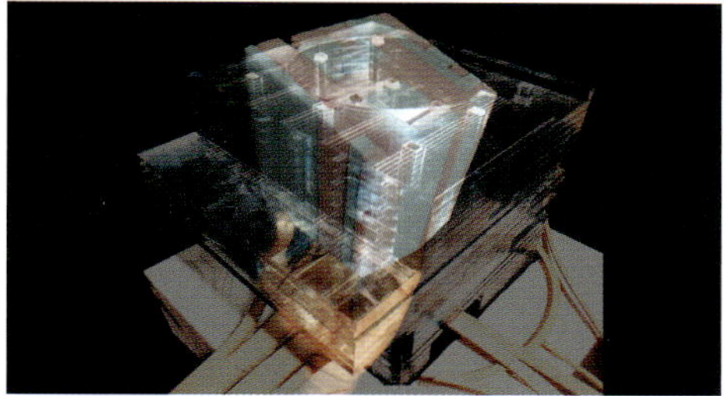
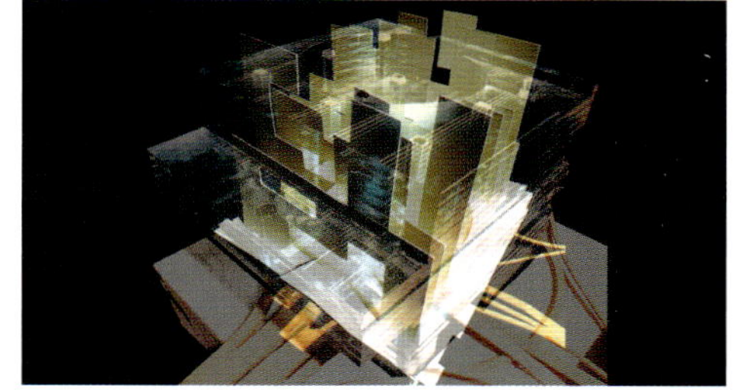

And by accepting these gifts, the poor and middle classes
All effectively became Ms. Winfrey's subjects.
The people had neither willingness, nor ability,
To separate their fates from Hers.

The ruined and corrupted public education system came next.
Her scholarship endowment of the University of Illinois at Chicago
Made college nearly free to all citizens of the state
For the foreseeable future.
U.I.C. was renamed the Chicago Free University.

Ms. Winfrey also built what by all measures
Was the world's largest charter school.
She provided a place for every child living within the city,
She guaranteed widespread, total equality of education.
Every family, rich and poor, sent their children
Since Her school surpassed even the best private institutions,
Both in terms of resources and student achievement.

Her triumphs over the worst and most chronic urban problems
Earned Ms. Winfrey the nickname: Mother of Us All.
Her investments had a dramatic effect on the urban economy
In just a few years.
The number of skilled employees began to multiply exponentially
As Chicago Free University expanded its enrollment
And people from around the world were attracted
To the prosperity and culture of wellness that She created.
Ms. Winfrey's empire grew as Her followers grew,
And the Central Area became Her company town.

The architect Daniel Burnham dreamed of the White City,
And his dream was finally realized
Upon the foundations of Ms. Winfrey's stewardship.
After Her hostile takeover of Google in 2025,
The OM library over the Circle Interchange
Became the undisputed center
Of global knowledge and communication.
This archive and its sister institutions renewed Chicago
As a center of enlightenment and spirituality
On the level of Vatican City or Mecca.

And thus, it was:
The Oprah ascended from icon to guru to prophet,
By building a Radiant City
Of inescapable benevolence,
Boundless wealth,
Relentless beauty,
And transcendent power.

Fig. 2: In Marshall Brown's First City scenario the nation's capital moves to Chicago after Washington, DC, is inundated by three hurricanes in five years. *Drowning Monument*, 2013. Collage on paper, 7" x 7".

Introduction

—

Karen Kice

Marshall Brown crafts visions for the future by remixing the material legacy of modern architecture. His reading of architectural history is discursive— a field of recurring ideas reenacted and reconstituted for different times and far-ranging locations. In other words, recurrence acknowledges that throughout architecture's history, many ideas—especially evocative ones—reappear. In Michel Foucault's *The Archaeology of Knowledge and the Discourse on Language*, novel ideas are not a rupture from the past but include configurations of sedimentary layers of history.[1] Brown constructs his visions with this understanding, using history as a material to represent and establish the basis for his work. However, he asserts his authorship not just by developing concepts in drawings, models, and collages but also by occasionally inserting himself. Glimpses of his hands, body, and silhouette appear in Brown's project films, which aligns with Foucault's description of the painter in Diego Velázquez's *Las Meninas* (1656) in *The Order of Things: An Archaeology of the Human Sciences*.[2] [Fig. 4] The painter appears in his own creation— not as a portrait but as part of the composition. The painter inhabits the world of his painting, similar to how Brown, the architect, inhabits the world of his architecture. [Fig. 5]

The triad of projects—UNITY Plan, Dequindre Civic Academy, and Smooth Growth Urbanism®— in this book represents more than fifteen years of development in Brown's architecture practice. They reveal his continued belief in architecture's power to enable improved relationships between the one and the many by giving shape to the civic realm. Brown also maintains that conventional architectural practice has a flawed relationship with time: too driven by present-day demands and ill-equipped to cope with the unpredictability of the future where any building may eventually be realized. Instead, he imagines future worlds, embracing uncertainty and opening his thinking to a multitude of realities. Though grand in scale and formally ambitious, the worlds he imagines allow for multiple possibilities. Rather than designing for a singular, desired future, Brown interrogates present-day realities and moves quickly beyond their limits into expansive scenarios that could exist years or decades from now.

Utilizing visionary thinking and representational techniques, Brown constructs experimental narratives with tools borrowed from the worlds of scenario planning and speculative fiction to develop what he calls "scenario spaces." This multidimensional framework begins with questions in the form of "What if…?," which become building blocks for plausible and divergent narratives. Brown's scenarios do not dictate the formal, spatial, or material characteristics of his architecture, but they do articulate worlds within which any design could plausibly exist. Scenarios propel his thinking across space and time, suggesting combinations and situations that might not be immediately apparent and, most importantly, that do not emerge from a linear sequence of causes and effects. [Fig. 3 and Fig. 12]

Center of the World, a 2010 scenario-building experiment, perhaps best illustrates this methodology. Brown created three short films that each propose a different future for the Chicago Circle Interchange— the unrealized site of Daniel Burnham's Civic Center in his 1909 *Plan of Chicago*.[3] [Fig. 6] The extreme scenarios challenge us to suspend disbelief, stretching our comfort zones beyond the expectations and boundaries of present-day assumptions. The scenarios also allow Brown to eschew didactic architectural descriptions in exchange for nonlinear fictions that build worlds capturing the complexities and possible

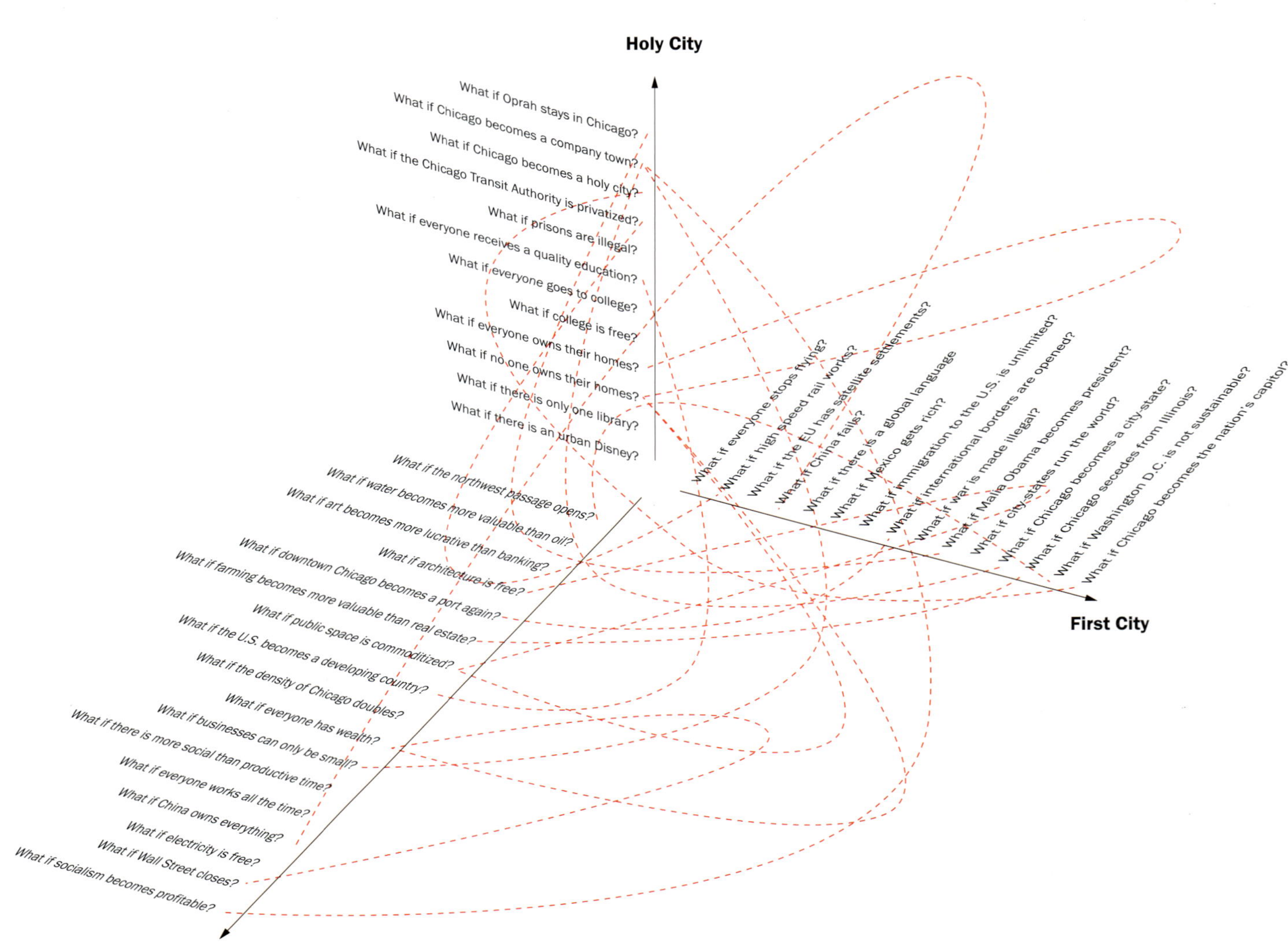

Fig. 3: The multidimensional geography of Brown's scenario space is constructed using plausible and divergent futures. The red dotted lines trace discrepancies within and among the narrative trajectories. For Brown, these discrepancies are productive errors that encourage creative negotiation among competing narratives. Scenario Space Diagram, Center of the World, 2010. Digital diagram.

Fig. 4: Diego Rodríguez de Silva y Velázquez, *Las Meninas*, 1656. Oil on canvas.

Fig. 5: Brown appears throughout the film for the Dequindre Civic Academy. In this still, his hand holds one of the thick, cloven columns that support the colossal building, while a portion of his masked face appears in front of the model of the school. Brown uses his hands—both literally and figuratively—throughout his work to create the drawings, models, and collages that index his thinking and record the struggle to translate ideas into architecture. He asserts his authorship with these images as evidence. *Dequindre Civic Academy*, 2016. Video still.

relationships between cultural, political, and economic forces behind large-scale urban interventions. Holy City foretells the transformation of Chicago after Oprah Winfrey's transition from media icon to guru to prophet. First City imagines Chicago as the next home for the nation's capital after Washington, DC, is repeatedly inundated by hurricanes. [Fig. 2] And CSSE (Chicago Socialist Stock Exchange) anticipates the rise of a financial center based on social enterprise after the 2009 global financial crisis. While Brown asserts that each of these scenarios is plausible in theory (e.g., there is a long history of guru-centered intentional communities, and Oprah already has a cultlike following), the scenarios are not predictions. Rather, they create a space for him to design with specific cultural, political, and social conditions in mind. Each film is a future history looking back to our present day, narrated by a computer-generated voice in a documentary style designed to encourage suspension of disbelief. Drawings, models, and collages are interspersed with maps and historical images to construct a view of future events. Intentionally conflating the past and future, these stories—which have become fundamental to Brown's practice—assist him in thinking across time and exposing the blind spots that constrain strategic thinking in the present. [Fig. 8] The move toward futurism was provoked by Brown's experiences designing the UNITY plan, an alternative master plan to a developer-driven scheme for the Brooklyn Vanderbilt Rail Yards. As an insurgent urbanist, Brown and the Atlantic Yards Development Workshop leveraged political divisions and competing interests by designing with the uniquely dynamic local conditions.[4] Brown challenged the prepackaged developer-driven scheme and gained an understanding of the shortcomings inherent in the typical, relatively passive roles of architects within urban development. The Yards taught him that to have real agency or make substantive change, architecture cannot be limited to the service of present-day demands from its myriad constituencies. Architecture takes time and, by definition, always exists in the future. Therefore, the ability to think years or decades ahead, depending on the scale or complexity of the vision, expands the agency of an architect. In his essay, "In the Seam," Joseph Becker outlines the complex social and political context that surrounded the UNITY plan, identifying how the political contestation had a substantive impact on Brown's architectural design process. Becker also parallels UNITY's

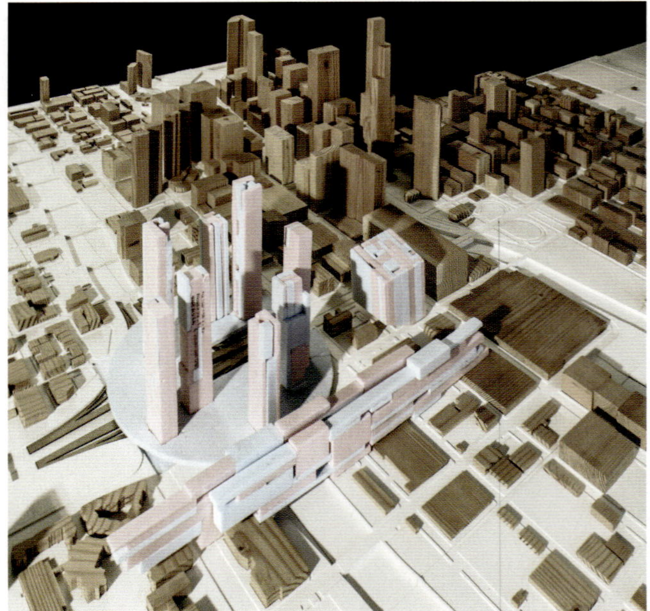

Fig. 6: A view of the Chicago Circle Interchange from the Sears Tower (now Willis Tower), looking southwest, captures what Brown describes as "a hole in the heart of Chicago." Chicago Circle Interchange, ca. 2013.

Fig. 7: In his vision for Holy City, Brown inserts a series of towers on a circular plinth atop the Chicago Circle Interchange. The foam models represent the OM (Oprah Media) Center, Great Library, and OM Housing, as a center of the world. Holy City model, Center of the World, 2010. Mixed media, scale: 1" = 50'.

seaming of the urban fabric to Brown's collage practice—skillfully constructing worlds by stitching together real urban sites with elements mined from the history of modern architecture.

Collage is more than a representational method for Brown: it is also a conceptual device where he uses history as a medium—cutting images and ideas from architectural photographs and drawing reproductions that he recombines to create dynamic, hybrid spaces. [Fig. 9] He uses architectural history as a collective resource—strategically collaging existing architecture fragments onto his forms to represent conceptual and material intentions. Similar to the scenarios, the collages propose a nonlinear reading of history, where the space-time continuum of architecture collapses to bring previously unassociated and often contradictory architectural elements together in surprising and sometimes transgressive configurations. [Fig. 11] Collage is just as much about what Brown selects as what he leaves out. In his Smooth Growth Plan for Chicago's Washington Park, for example, he takes up where Frank Lloyd Wright's Broadacre City left off in the search for an "ideal" American urbanism. Broadacre City and

Smooth Growth are prototypical low-density master plans that rethink property ownership's role within the vast American landscape. Both urban schemas also attempt to deal with multiple scales, from urbanism down to architecture.[5] [Fig. 10] Contrary to Wright's tabula rasa scheme for Broadacre City, however, Smooth Growth is shaped by emergent patterns in the neighborhood's geography and land use. Brown creates an order for his plan by tracing between housing clusters and well-trodden, informal pedestrian routes, resulting in curvilinear microregions overlaid on Chicago's eighteenth-century Jeffersonian grid. In the short film *The New Country*, he crafts a scenario for Washington Park's reconstruction when after two centuries of failed urban planning, Chicago is destroyed by a flood. Brown's protagonist is Daniel Freeman, the fictional architect of the plan, whom Adrienne Brown (no relation) discusses in her essay, "The New Old Frontier," to uncover many of the embedded narratives of Smooth Growth. Freeman's story is also a collage, an alter ego, assembled from both real and fictional characters in film, history, architecture, and parts of Marshall Brown's own life. Because Freeman's story

Fig. 8: Perspective view of Oprah's Holy City over the Chicago Circle Interchange, with her Great Library in the foreground, left. Elements of significant institutional and religious architecture are combined to envision a center of enlightenment and spirituality on the level of Vatican City or Mecca. *Holy City #1, Center of the World*, 2013. Collage on inkjet print, 54" × 40".

Fig. 9: Process photograph showing a framework onto which Brown embeds concepts into architectural forms. Vanderbilt Tower (under construction), UNITY plan, 2009. Collage on inkjet print.

Fig. 10: The Jack Lamberson House is an example of Frank Lloyd Wright's Usonian House concept, which he created as a component of his Broadacre City plan. Similar to Brown's Smooth Growth project, both plans considered multiple scales from the urban to the architectural. In Wright's plan for the Usonian House, each home would be situated on one acre of property as part of his ideal American town plan. Frank Lloyd Wright, Jack Lamberson House, Okaloosa, Iowa, photographed between 1948 and 1969.

Fig. 11: Design is an act of selection, trial, and error. In his collage for the Chicago Socialist Stock Exchange, Brown tests various combinations of building elements in attempts to negotiate the competing demands of complex programming, diverse scales, high architecture, and urban reality. *Chicago Socialist Stock Exchange #3*, Center of the World, 2013. Collage on inkjet print, 36 ½" × 60 ⅛".

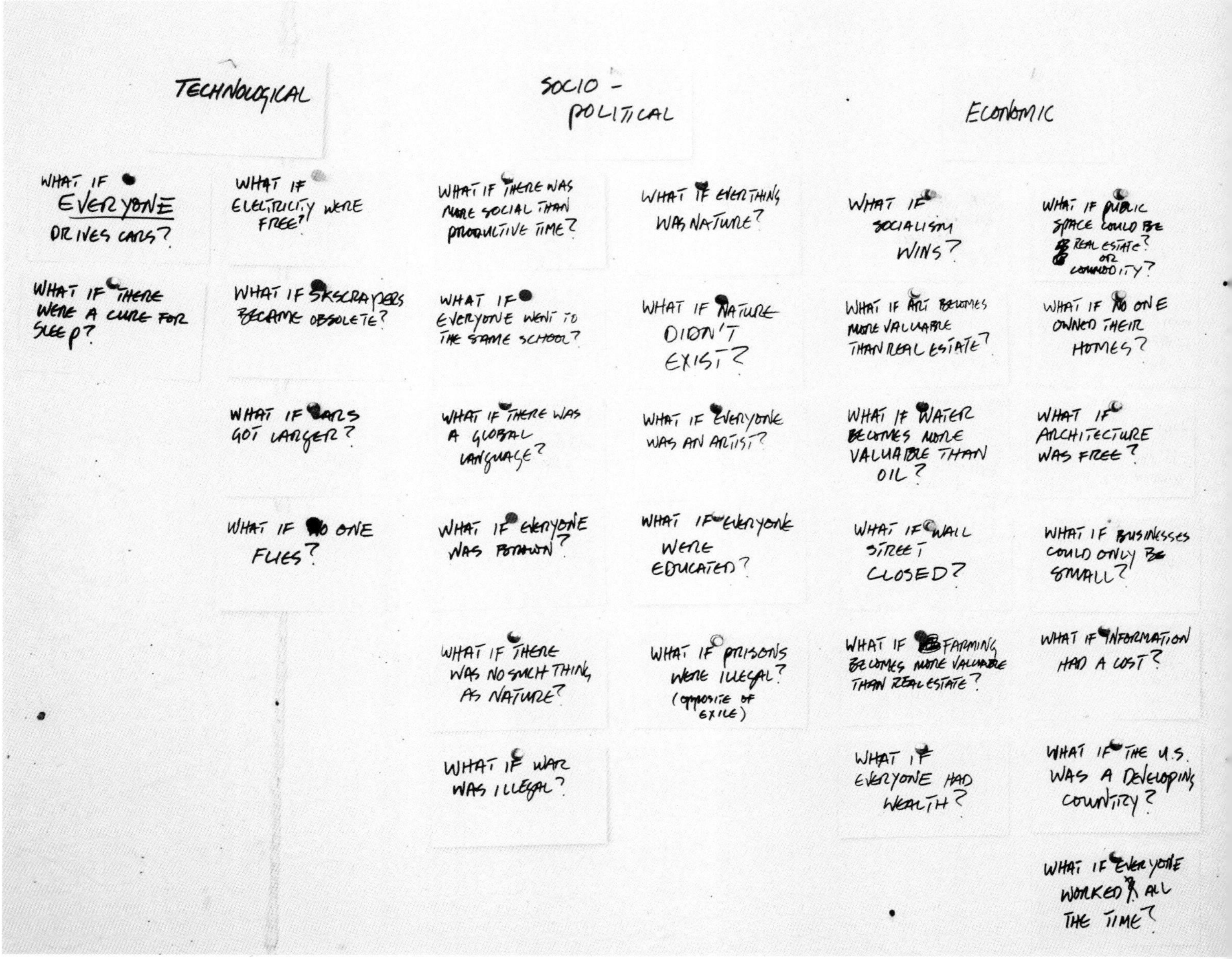

Fig. 12: A series of "What if…" questions is a device that Brown uses to build the scenarios to situate his architecture. *What if…?*, Center of the World, 2010. Ink on 4" x 6" index cards.

GEOPOLITICAL

WHAT IF CHICAGO WERE WASHINGTON D.C.?

WHAT IF THE EU HAD SATELLITE CITIES?

WHAT IF MICHELLE OBAMA BECOMES MAYOR?

WHAT IF IMMIGRATION TO THE U.S WAS ENTIRELY OPENED?

WHAT IF CITY-STATES RETURN TO PROMINENCE?

WHAT IF THE EU HAD A PERMANENT HOME NOT IN EUROPE?

WHAT IF THERE WERE NO INT'L BORDERS?

WHAT IF CHINA FAILS?

WHAT IF MEXICO GETS RICH?

WHAT IF CHINA OWNS EVERYTHING?

SPATIO-URBAN

WHAT IF CHICAGO WERE A STATE?

WHAT IF CHICAGO BECAME MOST POPULOUS CITY IN NORTH AMERICA?

WHAT IF THE DENSITY OF CHICAGO DOUBLES?

WHAT IF CHICAGO WERE THE WORLD'S LARGEST CITY?

WHAT IF THERE WAS A NORTHWEST PASSAGE?

WHAT IF CANADA GETS WARM?

WHAT IF CHICAGO WAS A PORT AGAIN?

WHAT IF THE LOOP SINKS?

WHAT IF THERE WERE COMPANY TOWNS (AGAIN)?

WHAT IF HIGH SPEED RAIL WORKS?

INSTITUTIONAL

WHAT IF URBANISM HAD A HOME?

WHAT IF OPRAH STAYS IN CHICAGO?

WHAT IF THERE WERE AN URBAN DISNEY LAND?

WHAT IF WAL-MART WAS URBAN?

WHAT IF THE CIA FAILS? (N.I.A.)

WHAT IF THE OLYMPICS HAD A PERMANENT HOME?

WHAT IF ARCHITECTURE HAD A HOME?

WHAT IF THE INTERNET HAD A HOME?

WHAT IF CHICAGO WERE A HOLY CITY?

WHAT IF COLLEGE WERE FREE? (C.F.U.)

WHAT IF THERE WAS ONLY ONE LIBRARY ANYWHERE?

is a patchwork, Adrienne Brown is able to situate him within the history of Chicago's South Side, filling in his biographical gaps and drawing his and Marshall Brown's vision closer to reality.

Throughout his work, Brown uses both design and nomenclature to envision landscape's potential as a collective resource and a key component for shaping twenty-first-century American cities. As in the collages, he manipulates spoken and written language to underline his intentionality and enhance comprehension of his speculative futures, thus increasing their plausibility. In Washington Park, he coined and later trademarked Smooth Growth Urbanism®, reinforcing his challenge to the contemporary fixation on densification as the main path to urban revitalization. In the same project, Brown rejects the term *vacant lot* for its pejorative associations with disinvestment and blight and instead optimistically insists that abandoned land is "available property."

The Dequindre Civic Academy, commissioned for the 2016 Venice Architecture Biennale,[6] demonstrates how Brown draws inspiration from modern architecture's material legacy to imagine a groundbreaking civic institution for Detroit. The architect John Portman's "coordinate unit" concept provides the precedent for Brown to formulate a city within the city.[7] In this nearly three-million-square-foot leviathan, Brown incorporates the complex histories of modern architecture in Detroit, from Portman's Renaissance Center to Ludwig Mies van der Rohe's Lafayette Park, into a single building with a civic scale and comprehensive program for an alternative mode of collective life. [Fig. 29] His quest to design a eutopian institution for the children of Detroit goes further to create a world within a city—a colossal incubator for every child from birth to adulthood.[8] Allison Glenn connects Brown's strategic mash-up of architectural ideas in her essay, "Like a Creature from Another Time," by pulling in references ranging from Chris Marker's film *La Jetée* to Detroit's culture of visionary techno music originators, the Belleville Three. She connects the formal inspirations of this monumental proposal to late modern megastructures, landscapes, and brutalist buildings. Glenn also poignantly recalls Gil Scott-Heron's lyrics to "We Almost Lost Detroit," reminding us of past failures and how much is at stake in the drive to keep Detroit alive while so many architects' visions attempt to take hold. The bittersweet tone of Heron's ballad

resonates with her own reservations of current development that disregards the unique history of Detroit. Glenn recalls her childhood experience in Portman's Renaissance Center as she analyzes Brown's ambitious program for a total environment dedicated to the well-being of the city's children and questions, if realized, what it would mean for the city.

By examining Brown's projects, *Recurrent Visions* interrogates the diverse sources and techniques he employs to translate ideas into architecture. Thinking for this book first began in Spring 2019 after an eponymous exhibition at Princeton University School of Architecture that used a thematic structure to present key concepts within an experiential format. While not all of the displayed works are published here, this book expands on the exhibition's concepts as they relate to three projects presented in their entirety. Together, these projects outline how Brown's visionary representations target the future yet are grounded in strategic reconfigurations of architecture's history placed in productive friction with contemporary urban realities. He reanimates the past to construct bold architectural visions that anticipate how we may navigate and inhabit worlds yet to come.

NOTES

1 Michel Foucault, "The Discourse on Language," in *The Archaeology of Knowledge and the Discourse on Language* (New York: Pantheon, 1971), 230.

2 Michel Foucault, "Michel Foucault: Las Meninas," in *The Critical Tradition: Classic Texts and Contemporary Trends*, by David H. Richter (Boston: Bedford / St. Martin's, 1998), 1222–23.

3 Daniel H. Burnham and Edward H. Bennett, *Plan of Chicago* (Chicago: The Commercial Club, 1909).

4 The Yards Development Workshop was formed in collaboration with then city council member Letitia James. Its members included Marshall Brown, Anna Dietzsch, Alex Felson, John Nafziger, and Sarah Strauss.

5 Wright developed his Usonian House; Brown has also proposed his Smooth Growth House as a prototypical American house for the twenty-first century.

6 This project was commissioned by Mónica Ponce de León and Cynthia Davidson for the exhibition *The Architectural Imagination*, in the US Pavilion for the 2016 Venice Architecture Biennale.

7 As defined in Allison Glenn's essay "Like a Creature from Another Time," Portman's coordinate unit is "a hybrid structure that houses the diverse programs of a city within a single utopic building."

8 Eutopian is not to be confused with utopian. Eutopian refers to a blessed or fortunate place versus the placeless, nonexistent, or ideal place that defines utopian. Lewis Mumford's essay "The Foundations of Eutopia" has been influential on Brown's thinking, which relates to his use of this term. See Mumford, "The Foundations of Eutopia," in *The Lewis Mumford Reader* (New York: Pantheon Books, 1986), 217–27.

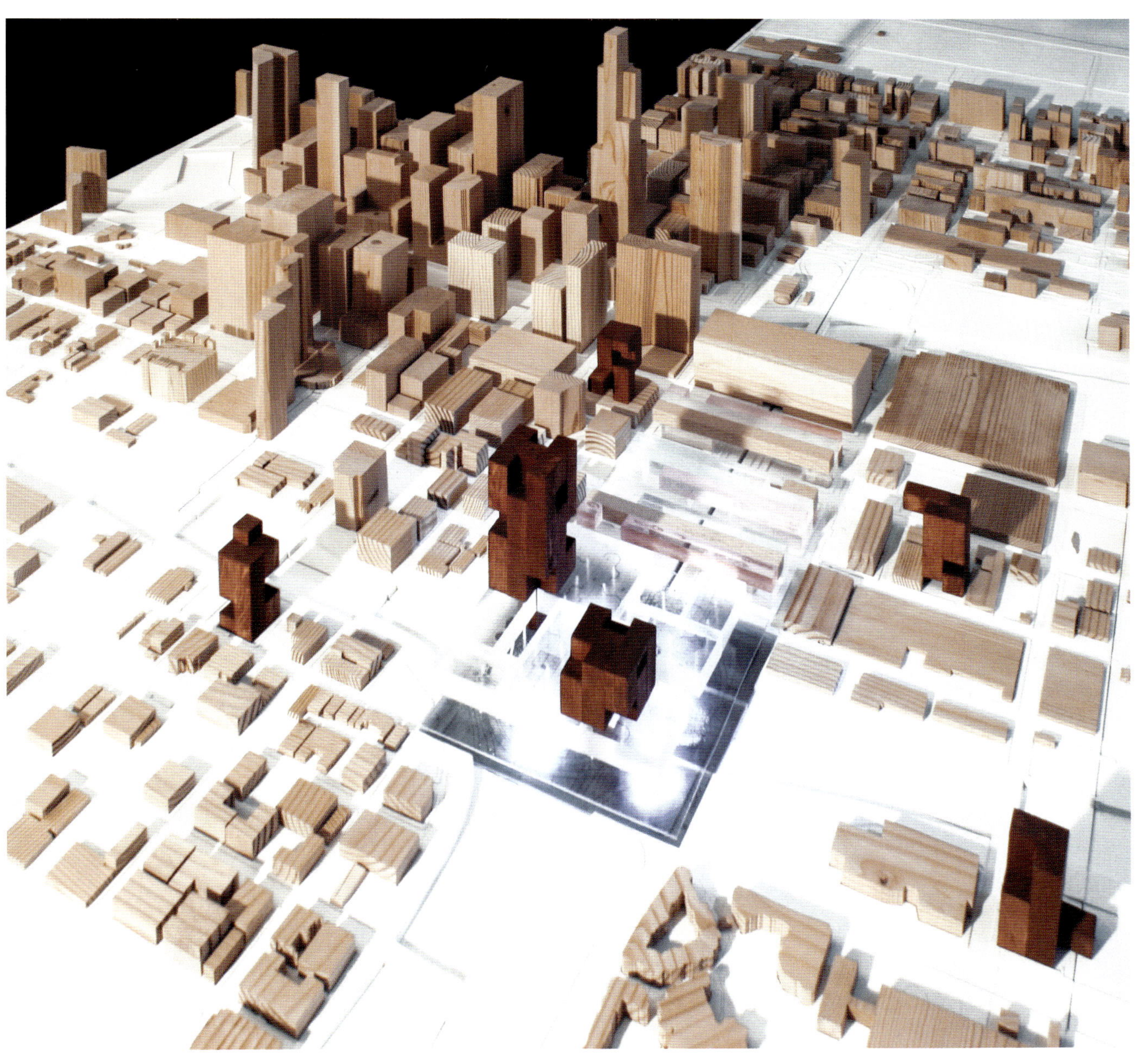

Fig. 13: The trading plaza glows
beneath the CSSE, a new center of the
world in Chicago. Wood, paint, and
acrylic. Center of the World model,
2013. Scale: 1" = 50'-0".

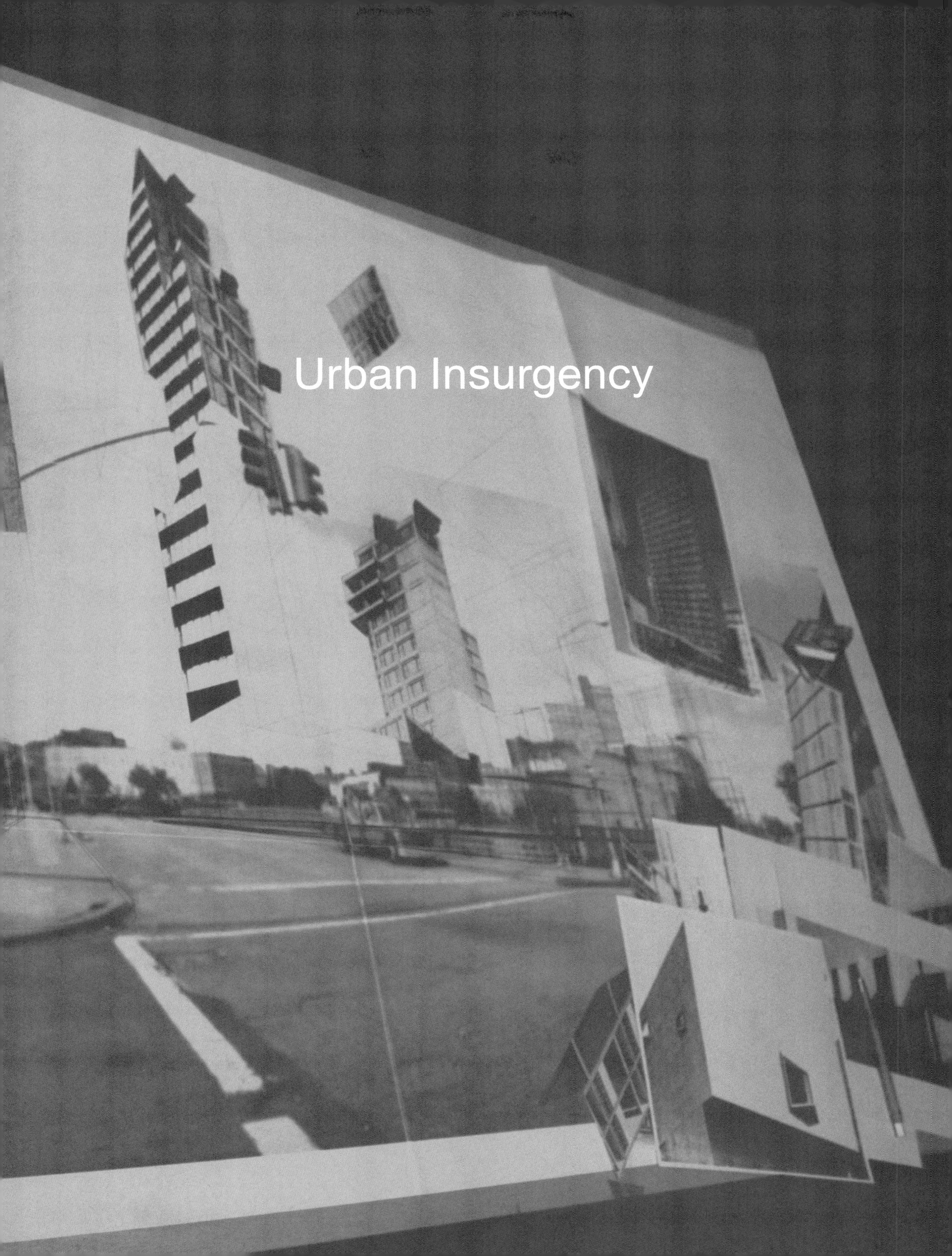

Urban Insurgency

Urban Insurgency
UNITY Plan, Brooklyn

The UNITY Plan for the Vanderbilt Rail Yards in Brooklyn establishes
a landscape of difference: a complex space where the competing demands
of real estate development, politics, urban culture, and architecture
are negotiated. Created as an alternative to the 2003 Atlantic Yards
proposal by Frank Gehry for Forest City Ratner Companies, this master
plan expanded the conversation around the site by engaging local politi-
cians, residents, and business owners. UNITY stands for *understanding,
informing, and transforming the yard*, and represents the urgent need for
an intelligent strategy that could produce a compelling vision for the
city's future. Located at the cultural epicenter of Brooklyn, the eight-
acre Vanderbilt Rail Yards is connected to the Metropolitan Transit
Authority Atlantic Terminal and separates the desirable neighborhoods
of Prospect Heights, Fort Greene, Park Slope, and Boerum Hill. UNITY
Plan is an episode in the long, contested history of the area. Beginning
in the 1950s, the Vanderbilt Rail Yards became the site of several
urban renewal projects—a few of which were realized, but many of which
failed, leading to the creation of the Atlantic Terminal Urban Renewal
Area in 1968.

With three large city blocks strung end to end, the Yards creates
an imposing gulf, making it difficult to cross between neighborhoods.
UNITY bridges the gap and creates connectivity between Prospect Heights
and Fort Greene by extending adjacent streets through the Yards. By
increasing connectivity, UNITY also creates more lot frontages and eight
smaller blocks. The greater number and smaller scale of these blocks
lay the groundwork for a richer environment with more diverse participa-
tion by developers, architects, and citizens. The Yards occupies a portion of what had been the location of André Parmentier's Horticultural
and Botanical Garden in the early 1800s. Inspired by this ecological
legacy, UNITY establishes a network of public spaces lengthwise across
the site, weaving through the blocks and connecting back to surrounding
streets. Together with green roofs and rain gardens at various levels,

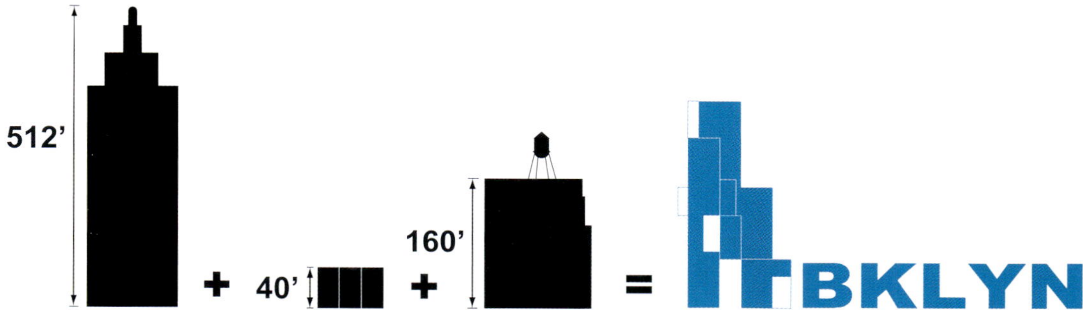

Fig. 14: Brooklyn has a diversity of densities, building sizes, and types. The UNITY Plan regulates building heights and massing to respond to these diverse conditions of warehouses, brownstones, towers, and big boxes throughout the area. Beyond the debate between brownstones and skyscrapers, UNITY posits a hybrid architecture that can accommodate and negotiate a heterogeneous and evolving context. Building Scales Diagram, UNITY Plan, 2007. Digital diagram.

these spaces in UNITY form an integrated stormwater management system from sky to ground, capturing and recycling water.

The Yards is the northern edge of a triangle that includes the Vanderbilt and Flatbush Avenue corridors. With the largest tower at the Atlantic Avenue and Vanderbilt intersection, the UNITY Plan rises in scale from west to east. This counterintuitive move is employed to increase activity at the east end of the site while relieving congestion at the west end with a new park over and around the Atlantic Terminal. Building heights and massing in the UNITY proposal respond to the diversity of densities, building sizes, and types found in Brooklyn and are designed to be regulated to respond to these diverse conditions—from brownstones and towers to warehouses and big boxes. To transcend the debate between low-scale development and high-end towers, UNITY sets the stage for a hybrid architecture that accommodates and negotiates a complex and evolving architectural context.

Fig. 15, overleaf: Brown uses collage as a method to select image fragments from architectural history as stand-ins for concepts that in combination with other fragments take on new meaning. He mines the knowledge and resources of architectural history to make explicit references. In this piece for UNITY, he fuses high-tech references from Jean Nouvel, Renzo Piano, and others alongside fragments of modern architecture including the Bauhaus, situated adjacent to landscapes by Carme Pinós and Álvaro Siza. This approach assumes that one architect doesn't design everything, similar to a master plan, but articulates strategies and establishes attitudes. Brown's collage technique also wages an implicit critique of digital rendering, which privileges photorealistic simulation. Collages, on the other hand, are abstractions that do not project final or realistic views yet still provide tangible visions of how architecture might appear in the world. Parmentier's Garden, UNITY plan, 2009. Collage and spray paint on inkjet print, 42" × 73".

Fig. 16: Outlined site of the MTA
Vanderbilt Rail Yards at the northern
boundary of a triangle that contains
Prospect Heights, Brooklyn. The
ellipse to the south is Grand Army
Plaza, the gateway to Prospect
Park. Aerial site digital photo of
Brooklyn, ca. 2007.

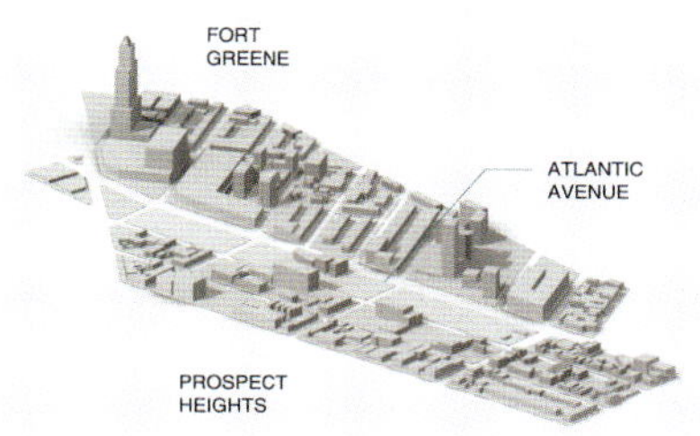

Current Separation
The MTA Vanderbilt Rail Yard is eight acres of fallow land that separates Prospect Heights, Fort Greene, Park Slope, and Boerum Hill. The Brooklyn Academy of Music, only two blocks away, attracts performers and visitors from around the world. Property values in all of the surrounding neighborhoods are skyrocketing.

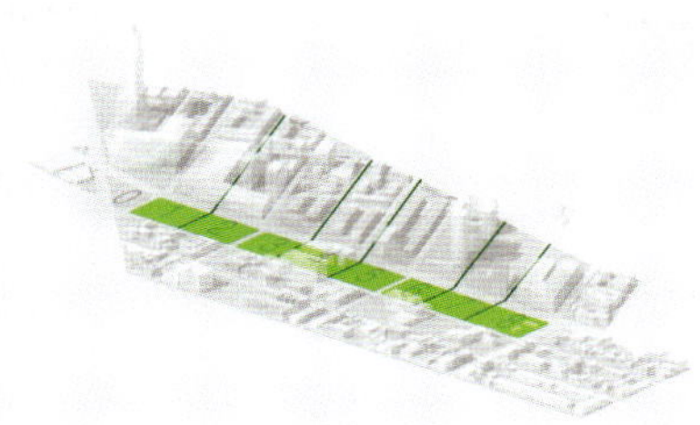

Make Connections
Instead of closing streets, we propose extending South Eliot, South Oxford, Cumberland, Adelphi, and Clermont into the Yards. The new streets create pedestrian connections and more lot frontages. They also create smaller sites that could be developed either simultaneously or gradually.

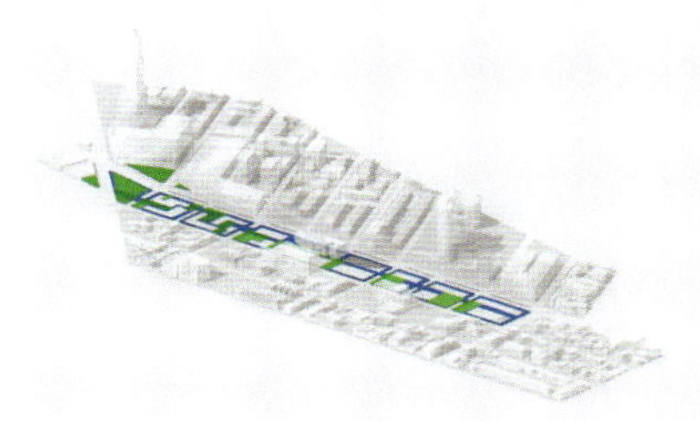

Brooklyn Is United
Instead of privately held courtyards, we have proposed a network of public spaces that would stretch the length of the site and connect to surrounding streets. This robust network of streets and open spaces will finally stitch the neighborhoods together.

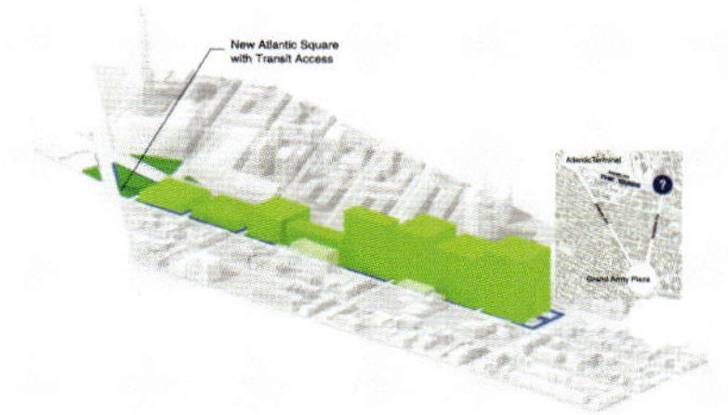

Distribute Density
The average proposed density for the Yards is Floor Area Ratio 7. The Yards form the northern edge of a triangle that includes the Vanderbilt and Flatbush Avenue corridors. Rather than increase the existing congestion around the Atlantic Terminal, we propose an alternative strategy that increases density at the Vanderbilt/Atlantic intersection. This will enhance that intersection and create the opportunity for a new park at the Atlantic Terminal similar to Union Square.

Integrate Scales
Beyond the debate between brownstones and skyscrapers, we have devised a hybrid architecture to accommodate and negotiate a heterogeneous and evolving context. Brooklyn has a diversity of densities, building sizes, and types. Building heights and massing in our proposal would be regulated to respond to these diverse conditions: warehouses, brownstones, towers, and big boxes.

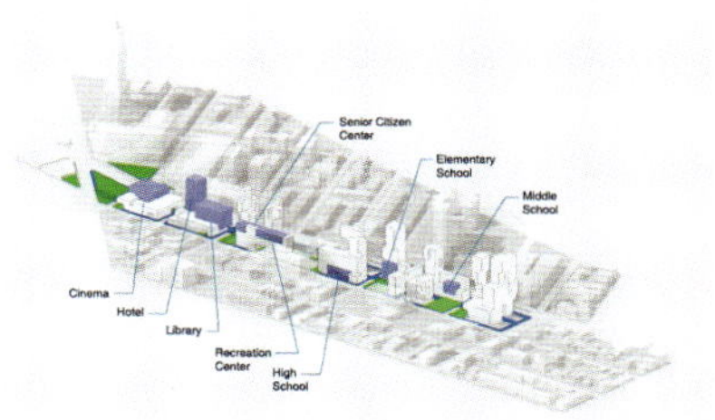

Diversify Development
Civic programs will be distributed along the entire Yards, completing the prototype for a stronger city of mixed-use, mixed income, and mixed culture.

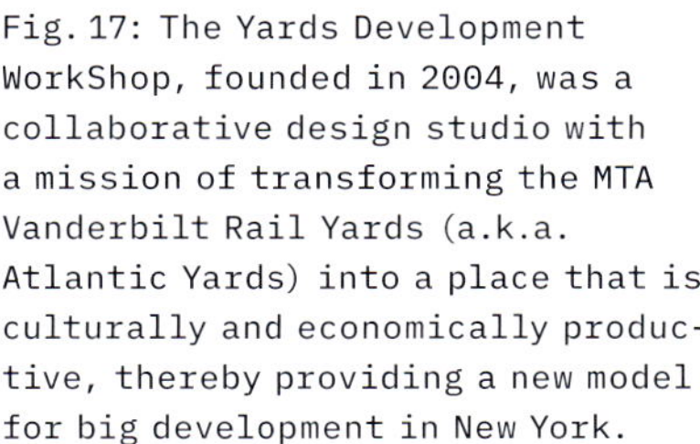

Fig. 17: The Yards Development WorkShop, founded in 2004, was a collaborative design studio with a mission of transforming the MTA Vanderbilt Rail Yards (a.k.a. Atlantic Yards) into a place that is culturally and economically productive, thereby providing a new model for big development in New York.

In cooperation with New York City Council Member Letitia James, our team of architects and urban designers from Brooklyn worked to create development alternatives for the Atlantic Yards—alternatives, of course, to the 7.6-million-square-foot proposal by Forest City Ratner Companies. These diagrams provide an an overview of our proposal, the UNITY plan for the MTA Vanderbilt Rail Yards.

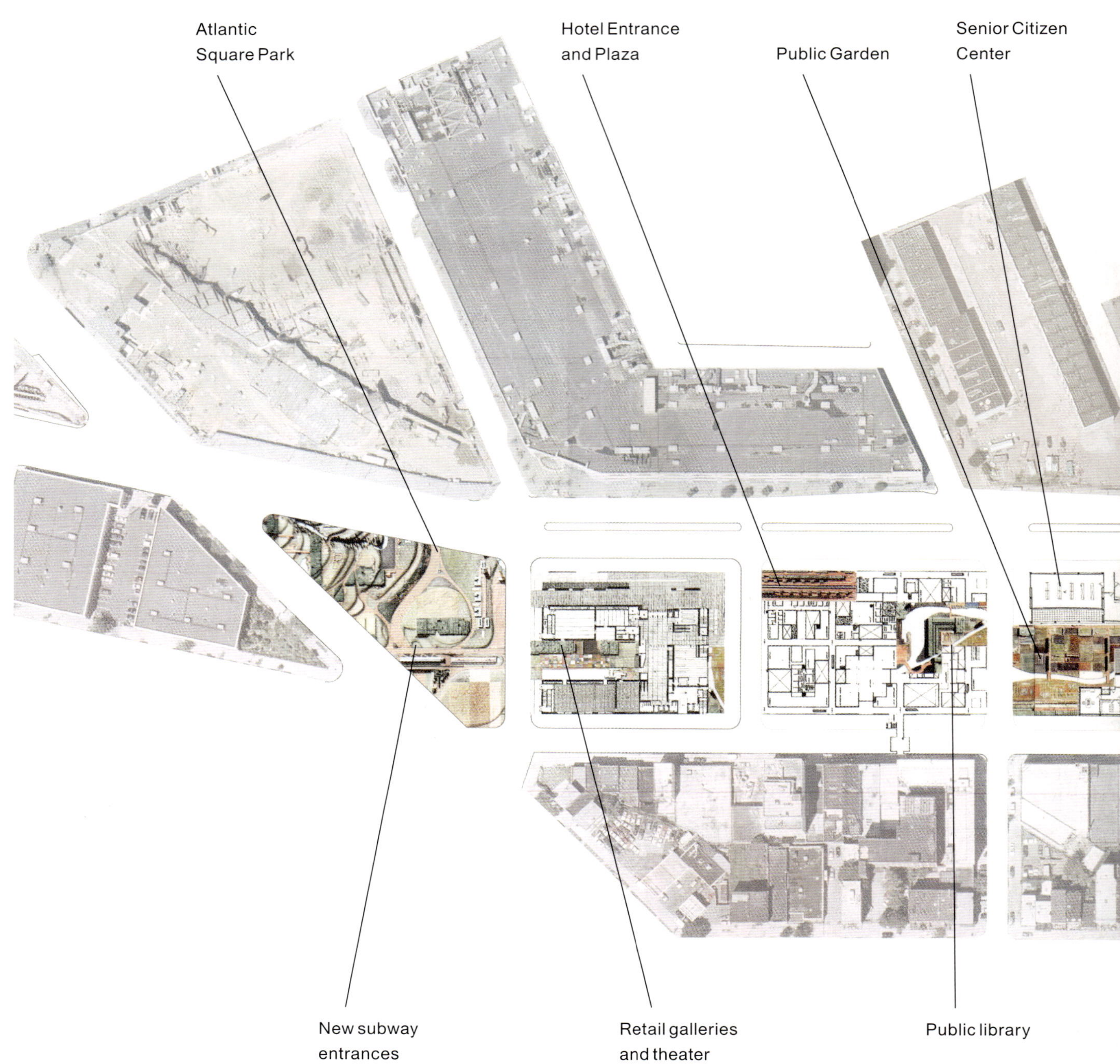
Atlantic
Square Park
Hotel Entrance
and Plaza
Public Garden
Senior Citizen
Center
New subway
entrances
Retail galleries
and theater
Public library

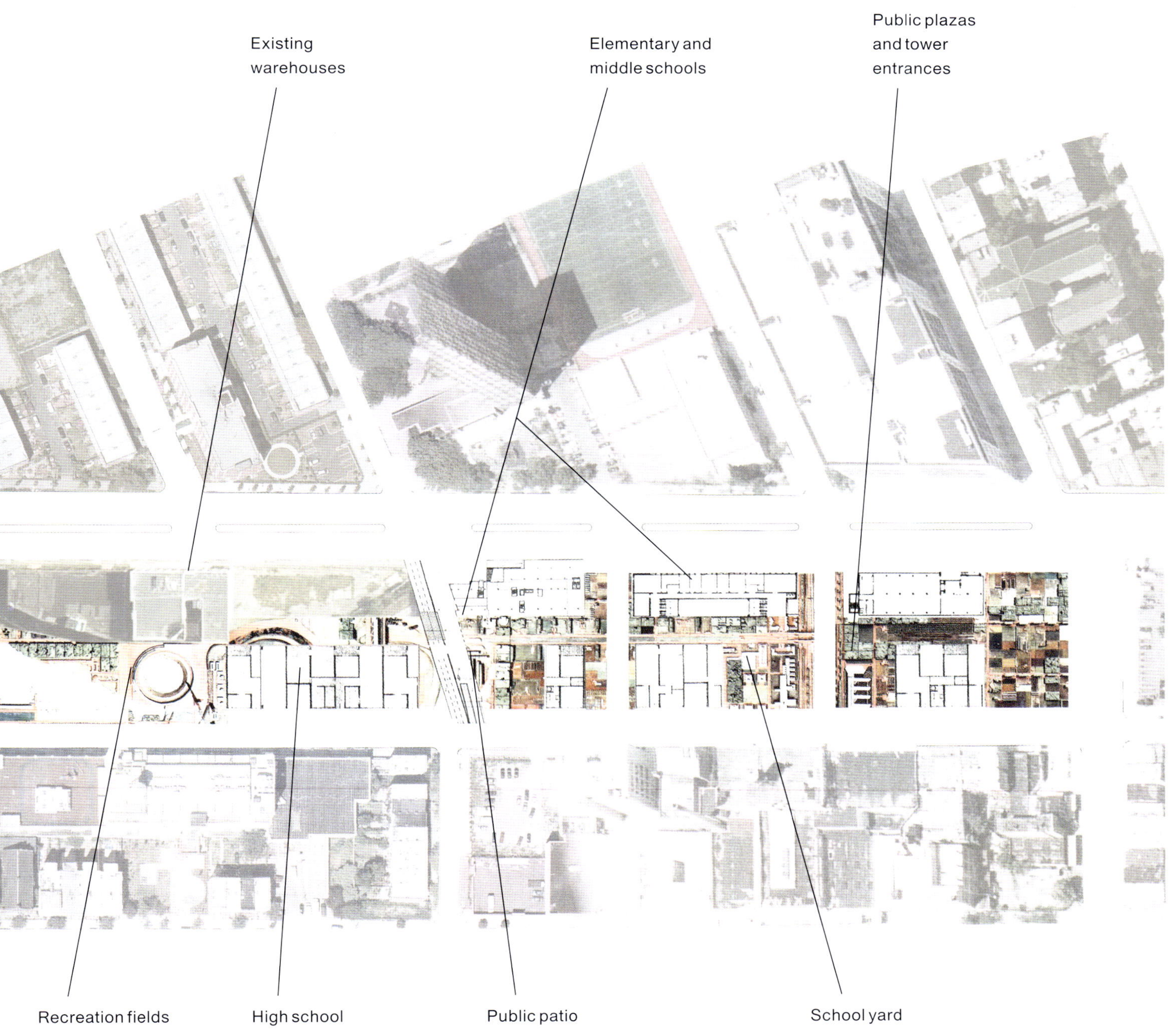

Fig. 18, above: UNITY creates a heterogeneous space where the incongruous demands of real estate finance, local politics, street culture, and high architecture can be negotiated. Modern and contemporary buildings are collaged with the landscape of Frank Lloyd Wright's Broadacre City to represent a possible ground plane for the entire site. *A Landscape of Difference*, site plan, UNITY plan, 2009. Digital montage diagram.

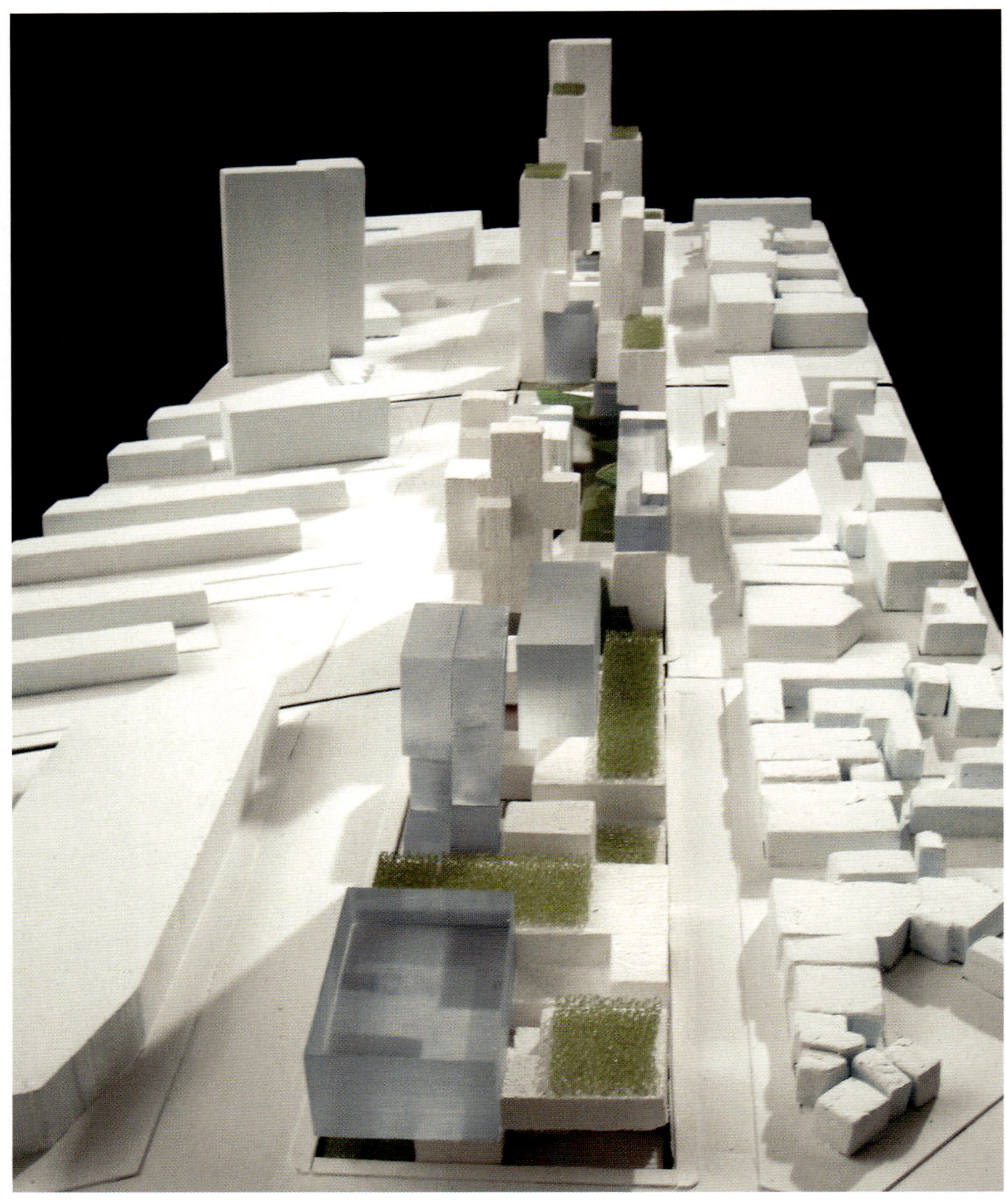

Figs. 19-20: Rather than increasing congestion around the Atlantic Terminal, UNITY adds density from west to east. A generous network of public open spaces is distributed throughout the site and connected by a pedestrian route composed of new interior paths and existing sidewalks. Model views looking east (above) and northwest (above right) toward the Williamsburg Savings Bank, UNITY Plan, 2009. Painted foam, sponge, and acrylic.

Fig. 21, previous: To the left, a new public library sits atop new retail spaces. To the right, a new tower with housing and senior citizens' center frames a public garden together with the new recreation center. *Sixth Avenue and Pacific Street*, UNITY Plan, 2009. Collage on inkjet print, 42" × 78".

Fig. 22, opposite: This tower at the corner of Vanderbilt and Atlantic Avenues is the tallest proposed building in the UNITY Plan. Two estranged progenitors of modern architecture are reunited in this collage—Mies van der Rohe and Le Corbusier. Mies's Seagram Building and Le Corbusier's Ronchamp chapel are transgressively juxtaposed within a single form. The fragments of the modern buildings become the flesh on the bones of this concept for a mixed-use tower in Brooklyn, New York. Juxtaposing the punctured mass of Ronchamp chapel with the minimalist curtain wall of Mies's Seagram Tower, the collage represents a mix of housing and commercial office programs. *Vanderbilt Tower*, UNITY Plan, 2009. Collage on inkjet print, 51" × 40".

In the Seam

—

Joseph Becker

In 2003, Forest City Ratner Companies unveiled the Frank Gehry–designed Atlantic Yards proposal for twenty-two acres of land extending from the Metropolitan Transit Authority Vanderbilt Rail Yards, a three-block void east of Downtown Brooklyn.[1] [Fig. 23] By promising a basketball arena, high-rise condos, affordable housing, and thousands of jobs, Bruce Ratner sold the eight-million-square-foot project as a "sweetheart deal" to the city and state—a massive urban renewal scheme wrapped with the allure of the starchitect in a bold public-relations wager.[2] Marshall Brown's UNITY Plan draws from the conflict and opportunity that emerged from critical responses to Ratner's project, and the understanding of the intersecting demands of the site, the politics, and the economy. Brown responded to the competing forces and conditions of Bloomberg-era New York by proposing an alternative vision—both an urban plan and a unifying set of tactics—with future implications for the built environment. UNITY's impetus stems from the disregard in Ratner's developer-driven model for the existing community and businesses, delivering a sobering lesson on the forces defining our urban progress.

The iterations on Gehry's designs for Atlantic Yards were a moving target, and Ratner's process was ill-fated from inception: rashly constructing a neighborhood where he assumed none existed when, in fact, a bourgeoning one already did.[3] Then city council member Letitia James's assessment of the plan described "a wall of skyscrapers, cutting off Prospect Heights from Fort Greene and Clinton Hill,"[4] asserting that "Ratner's buildings are going to divide my district and destroy the character of this community."[5] [Fig. 24] The proposal was for a massive, out-of-scale development, incongruous with the existing landscape. The site outline, however, was the most egregious offense—a land grab beyond the rail

yards predicated on threats to remove tenants and owners from their highly valuable homes and businesses by using eminent domain.[6] Gehry's plan was scrapped in 2009 after repeated cost-cutting revisions reduced the designs into obscurity, and the architect bowed out, heeding public blowback.

The critics' responses coalesced.[7] For Nicolai Ouroussoff, the project was a blunt-force effort to build at any cost, "no matter how thoughtless or dehumanizing the results. It is the kind of logic that kills cities—and that has been poisoning this one for decades."[8] And from Michael Kimmelman: the "Atlantic Yards project also exemplifies how the city, in this case hamstrung by the state, got planning backward, trying to eke public benefits from private interests awarded public subsidies and too much leeway."[9] Despite the promises to the community, Gehry's "ego trip" masterplan failed to engage and relate to the existing context adequately.[10] The process cut out the true stakeholders: the people of Brooklyn. Paul Goldberger underscored the blatant priorities: "Ratner seems to have been less interested in using Gehry's architectural talent to best advantage than in trying to leverage his celebrity to make an unpopular development more palatable."[11]

Contrary to Ratner's plans, it is a false choice between "getting it done" and "getting it done right." Developers, under the guise of "planning," too often prioritize margins and profits, operating without true consideration of the collectives, communities, and the urban collage built up over time. Through the creation of the Yards Development Workshop (YDW), Brown and James convened residents and designers to discuss the Atlantic Yards project's unvarnished details and implications. While embracing the idea of developing the site into a lodestone for Brooklyn, the YDW underlined the shortfalls of Ratner's proposal and established a forum for interest groups, voices,

Fig. 23, above left: The Yards sit at the intersection of Atlantic and Flatbush Avenues, two major Brooklyn thoroughfares. There is massive transportation infrastructure available to the site, but except for the daily passing of commuter trains, the MTA Vanderbilt Rail Yards lie mostly quiet twenty feet below the sidewalk. The Williamsburgh Savings Bank Tower is in the near distance, partially obscured by Forest City Ratner's previous developments: the Atlantic Terminal, Atlantic Center Mall, and an office building. The void of the yards holds the surrounding neighborhoods apart—a physical and experiential barrier. MTA Vanderbilt Rail Yards, 2005.

Fig. 24, above right: The impact of the new, potential development of the Atlantic Yards is depicted in this rendering of the proposed, large towers rising behind a photograph of the existing, relatively low-rise neighborhood. Photograph with digital rendering, 2006.

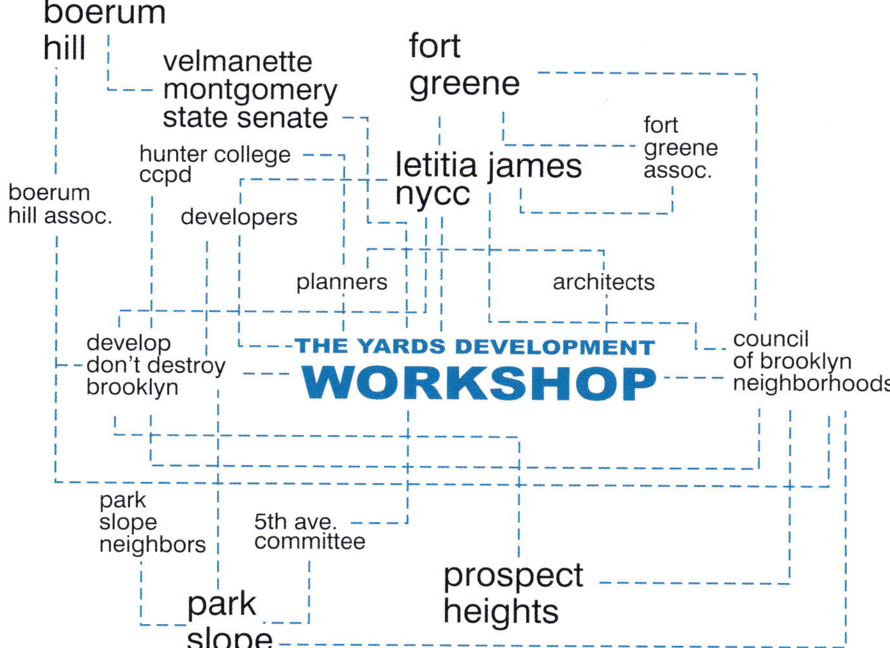

Fig. 25: In the Yards Development Workshop, civic engagement is reimagined as an open-source network allowing a wide range of voices and backgrounds. Unlike participatory planning that seeks consensus through design-by-committee, a diverse field of constituents with divergent and often competing agendas were engaged in public workshops that yielded ready-made ideas and information. Yards Development Workshop Network Diagram, UNITY Plan, 2007. Digital diagram.

and constituencies impacted by the development.[12] [Fig. 25] The UNITY Plan built on the YDW findings and was central to creating the "Principles for Responsible Community Development on the Vanderbilt Rail Yards,"[13] a guiding document for recentering the architectural process and focusing the proposal on the needs of the constituents beyond the sports arena and the housing quotas.

While not driven by community organizing, architecture as activism, or Jane Jacobs's people-first preservationism, Brown's UNITY Plan resonates with these moral and ethical ideals. There is a civic obligation underlying his efforts to draw out benefits of the often-discordant relationships between architecture and collectivity, and power structures that produce and sustain them both. For Brown, there is a stark difference between consensus among these forces and the rich potential of their productive conflict. The Brooklyn neighborhoods surrounding the Vanderbilt Rail Yards are both enclaves and melting pots, blending smoothly or abutting conspicuously, but held apart by the yards. [See Fig. 18] This gap is bridged in UNITY, which was rendered mostly in collage and massing models, fitting tools for connecting the urban

fabric's discrete elements. Particularly in the collages, each architectural element is carefully and cautiously seamed with the same attention Brown applies to stitching together the city itself.

Collage emerged from UNITY into a crucial through line of Brown's practice. His assemblages combine elements of iconic works of architecture and urbanism into new, imagined landscapes. They index his references while serving as research and representation. In UNITY's Vanderbilt Tower [See Fig. 22], dismantling and reassembling modernist heavyweights like Le Corbusier and Mies van der Rohe present a fortuitous juxtaposition. The sensuous movement of the Ronchamp chapel placed in tension with the cold rationalism of the Seagram Building becomes a stand-in for the poetic interplay the site necessitates. The tower exists in the seaming of these aesthetics and ideas, an entirely "other" entity emerging out of the sum of the parts. Brown establishes collage as a tool of communication, connection, contextualization, and coexistence.

The UNITY project and the experiences informing and directing the YDW have helped shape Brown's practice and his architectural and procedural

Fig. 26: The Yards Development Workshop was conceived as an exercise in civic education and engagement. This document was designed to be a primer covering the physical characteristics, geographic conditions, political boundaries, and history of the area surrounding the MTA Vanderbilt Rail Yards. It was used as a basis for discussion between design professionals and residents at the first workshop on March 20, 2004.

The Yards Development Workshop Brochure by Marshall Brown, Sarah Strauss, and John Nafziger, 2004. Print on paper, 17 ½" × 52 ½".

philosophy, and the idea that if we can change the way we think, we can change the way we build. It was, first of all, an information campaign, demonstrating a design process that could engage disparate parties and their competing, adjacent, and enmeshed needs. [Fig. 26] Responding to the Atlantic Yards proposal, Michael Sorkin, the architect, advocate, and crusader for the built environment, argued that the voice of the people could be in the service of constructive development.[14] He influenced Brown's practice in how he staked out an ethical position in architecture, explored the ideas of propinquity and adjacency, and worked within systems of power while critiquing them in a determined coexistence. Sorkin's tools— broad criticism, drawings, and collages—enriched Brown's deep understanding and incorporation of the complex political, architectural, and social issues at play in our real, lived, urban space. [Fig. 27]

Although there is no contradiction in planning both inductively and deductively, our process is too skewed toward money and away from people: the capacity of neighborhoods to meaningfully participate in planning their own destinies—and that of the larger realms we all share—is fundamental.[15]

These participating voices are crucial to an architect's understanding of contexts and conditions— not as a community's compiled desires or design-by-committee but recognizing that the final architectural result is a part of the fabric we share.

Fig. 27: This speculative proposal by Michael Sorkin for a housing project on Canal Street in Manhattan addresses the complexity of the urban site through the use of collage. Sorkin's hybrid architecture, a product of grafting the design into its context, exhibits similar ambitions to Brown's. *Sheep*, Michael Sorkin Studio, 1993.

Brown's position is not activist posturing but a desire to understand and renegotiate the dynamics of the architecture discipline, making room for meaningful change. By exploring these ingrained forces, Brown aims to circumvent the pitfalls of projects like Atlantic Yards. Architects who are intent on building always have to be reactive: responding to clients, to codes, and to financial and real estate markets. UNITY helped establish Brown's approach to architecture today: to actively think steps ahead, and even redraw the architectural process, beginning explicitly with the complex conditions of sites and competing voices to better facilitate smooth, conse-quential, and supportive growth.

Ultimately, what we build is a choice. Marshall Brown questions *who* makes these choices that generate such immense impact on our shared future. These priorities create our cities' lasting environments, which, for Brown, directly reflect our values.[16] In the void of the sunken yards, in the vacuum of creative vision, and in the seam of Brooklyn's fabric, Brown envisioned a suture between communities and a locus for new energy by drawing on what existed. To make good on our ideals—the combined cultural, social, and political principles for our ethical evolution—means thinking through the entire picture, advancing an ecological urbanism that preferences long-term goals over short-term gains,[17] treasuring public interest over private, and actively celebrating the beauty and richness in the seams of the urban fabric.

Fig. 28: The MTA Vanderbilt Rail
Yard in 2009. The photo is taken
from Atlantic Avenue, looking at
Carlton Avenue, one of the streets
removed as part of Forest City
Ratner's master plan.

NOTES

1   In 2014, it was renamed Pacific Park as part of the developer's rebranding, selling a majority share to Greenland USA, and forming Greenland Forest City Partners. The new estimated completion date is 2035, though the below-market "affordable" units are due by 2025. At the time this was written in Spring 2021, nearly eighteen years after the original Ratner plan, the arena and four towers (of the originally announced sixteen towers) have been built, with four more towers under construction. Of the 2,250 "affordable" units, 782 have been built, with 592 under construction, and 876 more required. None of the initially promised ten thousand office jobs have emerged. The project, initially said to cost $2.5 billion, is now estimated to cost at least $6.6 billion.

2   Marshall Brown, "Not Good, but Well Behaved," in *Block by Block: Jane Jacobs and the Future of New York*, ed. Timothy Mennel, Jo Steffens, and Christopher Klemek (New York: Municipal Arts Society of New York; Princeton Architectural Press, 2007), 33.

3   Norman Oder, "Atlantic Yards / Pacific Park Report," accessed March 12, 2021, atlanticyardsreport.blogspot.com.

4   Letitia James was a first-term city council member at the time, elected after her predecessor James E. Davis was assassinated by a political opponent in New York City Hall in 2003. She later became a crusading public advocate for the City of New York, and is now New York State's attorney general, notable for suing both the National Rifle Association and Donald J. Trump.

5   Ariana Speyer, "Letitia James," *Index Magazine*, Summer 2005, http://www.indexmagazine.com/interviews/letitia_james.shtml.

6   The development's eminent domain abuses are covered in the 2011 documentary *Battle for Brooklyn*, by Michael Galinsky and Suki Hawley. The story follows Daniel Goldstein, the last holdout resident.

7   Although the *New York Times* was slow to criticize, perhaps because Ratner was the development partner on the Renzo Piano–designed Times Tower (2003–7).

8   Nicolai Ouroussoff, "Battle between Budget and Beauty, Which Budget Won," *New York Times*, June 8, 2009, https://www.nytimes.com/2009/06/09/arts/design/09arena.html.

9   Michael Kimmelman, "An Arena as Tough as Brooklyn. But Street Smart?," *New York Times*, October 31, 2012, https://www.nytimes.com/2012/11/01/arts/design/barclays-center-arena-and-atlantic-yards-project-in-brooklyn.html.

10   Jonathan Lethem, "Brooklyn's Trojan Horse," *Slate Magazine*, June 19, 2006, https://slate.com/culture/2006/06/an-open-letter-to-frank-gehry.html.

11   Paul Goldberger, "Gehry-Rigged," *New Yorker*, October 16, 2006, https://www.newyorker.com/magazine/2006/10/16/gehry-rigged.

12   Marshall Brown, "Back to the Garden: The Ecological Evolution of the Atlantic Yards," in *New Directions in Sustainable Design*, ed. Adrian Parr and Michael Zaretsky (London: Routledge, 2010), 56.

13   This document was authored and endorsed by several local organizations, including Develop Don't Destroy Brooklyn, the main opposition group to the Ratner proposal.

14   Michael Sorkin's passing in 2020, an early victim of the COVID-19 pandemic, was a loss to the architecture community and beyond. He was a tremendous influence on critics, designers, and urbanists, including Brown.

15   Michael Sorkin, "Bridge over Troubled Waters," *Architectural Record*, January 16, 2014, https://www.architecturalrecord.com/articles/6223-bridge-over-troubled-waters?v=preview.

16   Marshall Brown, "Driverless Cities," TEDxIIT, TEDx Talks, 2017, https://www.youtube.com/watch?v=RemvHyWTEa0.

17   Brown, "Back to the Garden," 56.

SMN STAGE

Coordinate Unit

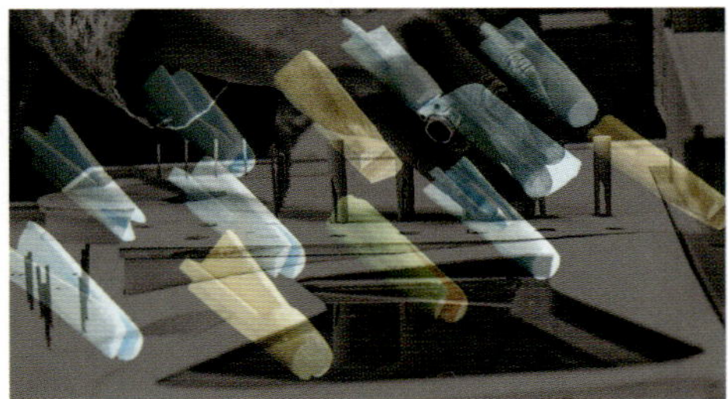
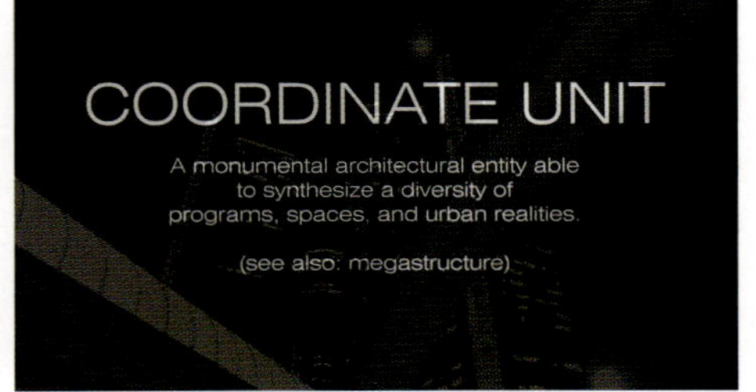

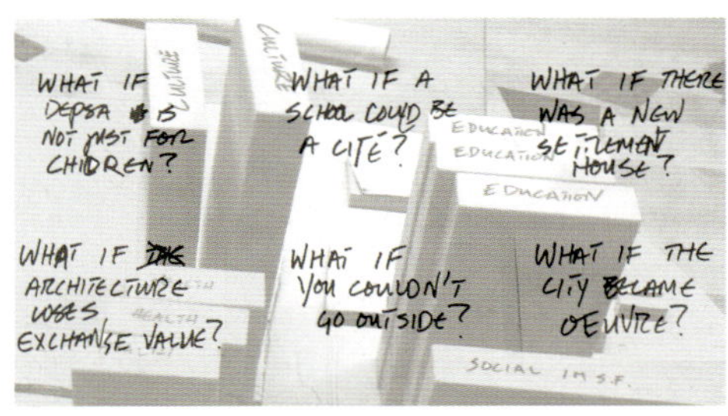

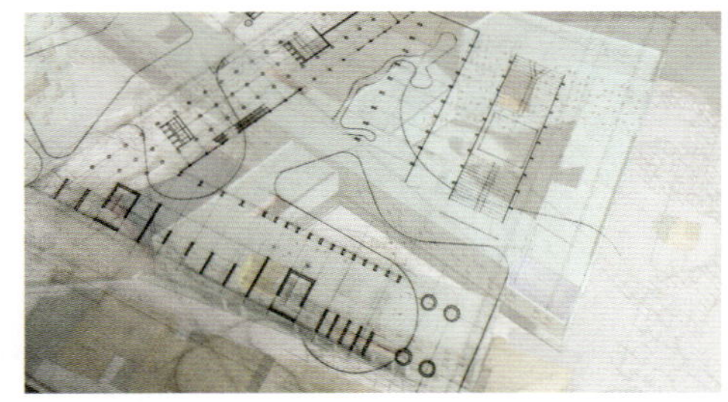

Detroit, May 21, 2026.
The Dequindre Civic Academy, the DCA,
Conducted opening ceremonies this week.

As part of the city's ongoing reconstruction,
The new institution, which grew out of the former
Detroit Edison Public School Academy,
Has dramatically expanded its mission and scale
By accepting responsibility for the physical, social,
Cultural, and intellectual development of the city's children
From birth to adulthood.

After decades of depopulation,
The city council hopes to expand the ranks
Of socially prepared and intellectually equipped citizens
By privatizing the school system.

DCA was conceived as a citadel
That will shelter its pupils from the shocks
Of Detroit's ongoing transformation
While also inspiring visions for a metropolitan future,
A future that still remains uncertain.

DCA is more than a school.
The architect imagined it as the physical manifestation
Of America's motto: e pluribus unum, out of many, one.

The entire 2.7-million-square-foot facility
Is a coordinate unit, a single architectural entity
Able to synthesize many diverse programs and spaces.
The idea of the coordinate unit was developed earlier
By John Portman, architect of Detroit's Renaissance Center.
In his 1976 book, *The Architect as Developer*
Portman describes it as a total environment
In which practically all of a person's needs are met,
A village where everything is within reach of the pedestrian.

The architecture of DCA is also a total environment
With enough space and all the facilities necessary
For its inhabitants to thrive.
The megastructure's main spine,
Bridges the Dequindre Cut, just south of the school's former location,
And forms a new gateway connecting Detroit's Eastern Market
With the outlying territory.

DCA is a monumental concrete structure
Which has been tinted with green calcite aggregate.
Four-foot-thick exterior walls with large,
Deeply set windows insulate the interior
From the increasingly extreme summer heat and winter cold.

The vertical west wing contains additional public programs,
Including cultural spaces, a community college,
Workshops, and apartments for faculty.
The taller tower measures 865 feet, with a bronze-clad volume
Housing a worship center near the top and an observatory on the roof.

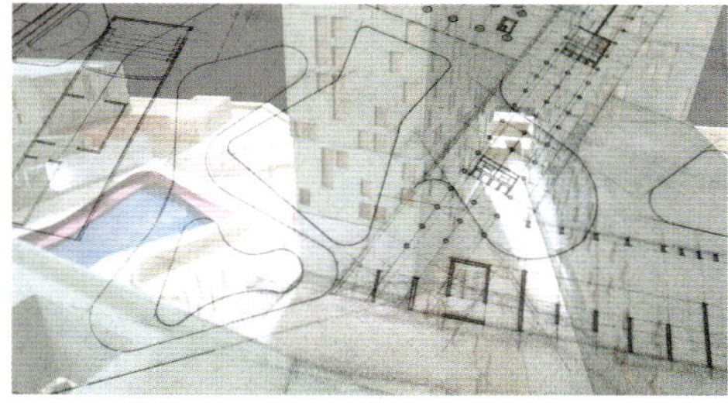 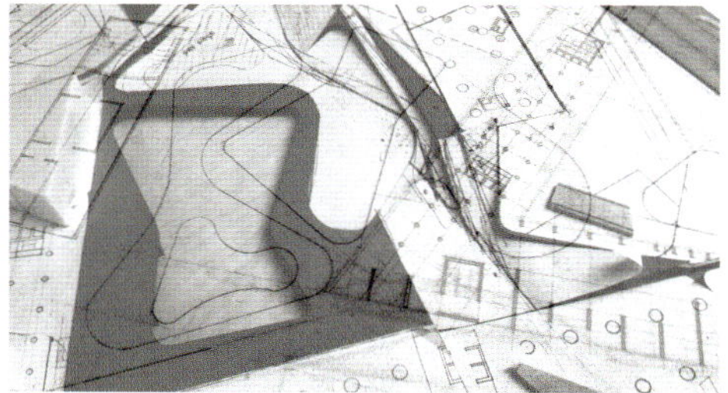 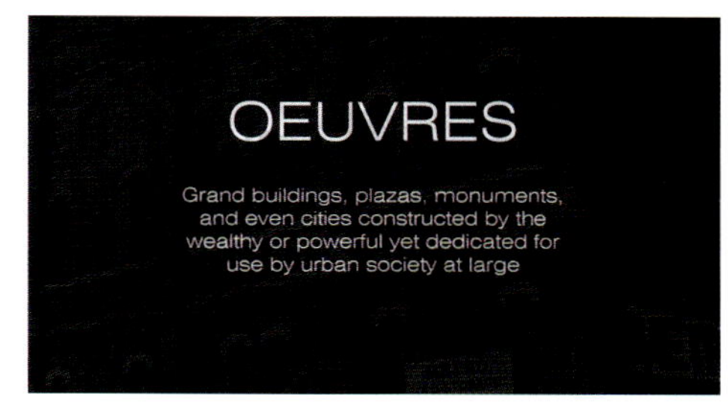

  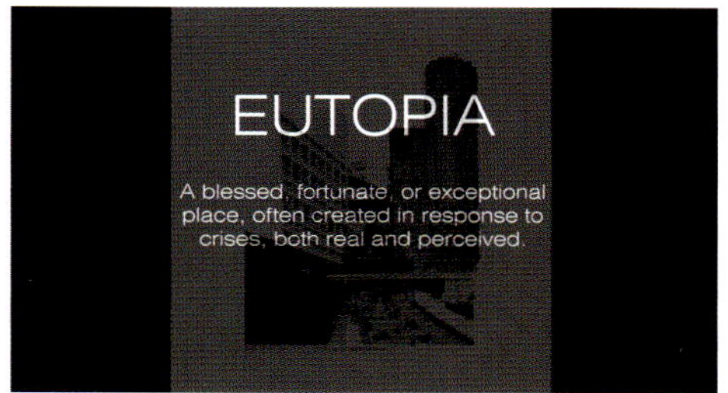

The lower wing across the Cut
Is set among the quiet pastures of East Detroit.
It contains family apartments, dining halls, a clinic,
The recreation center, and library.
Both the east and west wings embrace large outdoor patios
With strategically placed thresholds that provide security
While also creating formal entries to the complex.

A third public patio set 20 feet below street level
Within the Dequindre Cut can be accessed
Via new pedestrian paths and bicycle routes.
A pond for summer swimming and winter skating
Is the centerpiece of the space where the school intersects
The public infrastructure of the Cut.

The academy's primary school hovers nearby,
Bridging diagonally between the southeast
And northwest corners of the building,
Connecting the site's urban and pastoral sides.
It is supported by a series of monumental cloven columns
split at their bases, allowing people to walk through
with a sense of ceremonial passage.

The philosopher Henri Lefebvre once wrote
That the Industrial Era destroyed urban society
By replacing oeuvres with products.
In twenty-first century Detroit, the decline of real estate
Has placed renewed attention on the use value of architecture
As civic infrastructure and aesthetic experience.

When DCA was first proposed in 2016,
Few believed that this kind of monumentally civic project
Could still be achieved in America.
Nonetheless, taking its place
Alongside Portman's Renaissance Center
And Mies van der Rohe's Lafayette Park,
DCA has established a new refuge for collectivity
In a landscape of growing isolation.

With the DCA, the architecture aspired to create a utopian institution,
A fortunate or blessed place, within Detroit,
Knowing as he did that architecture cannot solve society's problems,
But that it can formalize utopian models
That inspire civic life and eventually lead to
Greater and more beautiful urban worlds.

Coordinate Unit
Dequindre Civic Academy, Detroit

The Dequindre Civic Academy (DCA) imagines a new kind of school as it formalizes a visionary civic role for Detroit's privatized charter school system. Proposed as an expansion of the Detroit Edison Public School Academy, this 2.7-million-square-foot campus is a citadel designed to shelter its pupils from the city's ongoing and uncertain transformation. More than a school, DCA is a manifestation of America's motto, E pluribus unum—out of many, one. Like John Portman's Renaissance Center in Detroit, the building is a coordinate unit[1]—a single architectural entity that combines many diverse programs. As a total environment, the DCA contains enough space and all the facilities necessary for its occupants' welfare, including education, housing, health, and cultural uses.

Detroit's ongoing transformation inspires an embracing architecture including all the necessary programs for Detroit's children, its future builders, to thrive. DCA creates a physical bridge between two plots straddling the east and west banks of the Dequindre Cut—a two-mile pedestrian and bicycle path, converted from a former Grand Trunk Railroad Line and running along the bottom of a twenty-foot-deep trench. Likewise, it raises important questions about how to create civic spaces in negotiation between the public and private, the urban and the pastoral.

The building's central spine contains the primary school and runs diagonally from the southeast to northwest, connecting Detroit's bustling Eastern Market to the more pastoral East Side. [Fig. 29] A series of monumental cloven columns support the school, each split at its base and forming a ceremonial gateway between Detroit's center and the outlying territories. Four-foot-thick exterior walls tinted with green calcite insulate the interior from extreme weather, while large windows set deep into the facade provide spectacular city views. Public programs, including the galleries, auditorium, community college, workshops, and faculty apartments, are housed in the west wing. A black box theater, bronze-clad chapel, and rooftop observatory occupy the taller of two towers. Set among the quieter pastures of Detroit's East Side,

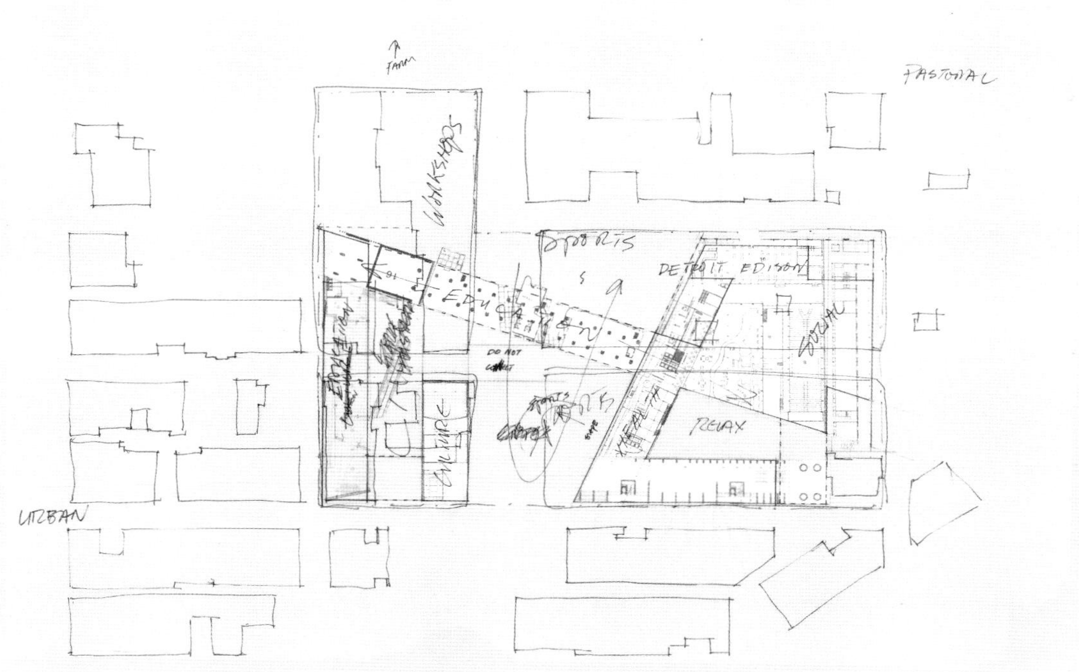

Fig. 29: Drawing with collage that represents Brown's early efforts to bridge the site's urban and pastoral sides using both program and architectural form. Cutting and pasting fragments of building plans from across modern and contemporary architecture allow him to quickly articulate the building's spatial qualities in relation to programs distributed throughout the campus. Site Plan Study, Dequindre Civic Academy, 2016. Ink and collaged photocopies on tracing paper, 24 ½" × 36 ¾", scale: 1" = 50'.

the opposing wing is lower and contains domestic programs, including family apartments, dining halls, a clinic, a recreation center, and a library. Both wings surround large outdoor patios flanked by thresholds that serve as formal public entries into the complex. A third patio with a pond is set twenty feet below, within the Dequindre Cut, and accessed by pedestrian paths and ramps.

In twenty-first-century Detroit, the decline of property values can reaffirm architecture's role as civic infrastructure and aesthetic experience. Alongside Portman's Renaissance Center and Mies van der Rohe's Lafayette Park, the DCA claims its place as a monumental collective refuge, standing astride a landscape of fragmentation and isolation. In neoliberal America, where the public and private spheres are increasingly and often problematically intertwined, this campus within a building reasserts the importance of public education as a civic institution by presenting a eutopian model for nurturing civic life—another city within the city.

NOTES

1   For more on the coordinate unit, see John C. Portman and Jonathan Barnett, *The Architect as Developer* (New York: McGraw-Hill, 1976), 128–43.

Fig. 30, above: Sketch articulating the outdoor spaces framed by the DCA by removing the building and focusing on the ground. The winding arrow describes movement through these landscapes over the course of a day, a week, or a lifetime. Landscape and Circulation Concept Plan, Dequindre Civic Academy, 2016. Ink and Prismacolor on tracing paper, 24" × 30".

Fig. 31, opposite: Bridging the Dequindre Cut, the DCA becomes a new refuge for collectivity in Detroit. This view looking south down the Cut shows the school bridge with the administrative and cultural towers just beyond. Combined fragments of brutalist architecture represent the DCA's connection to late modernist architecture's dream of creating cities within cities. *Toward a Coordinate Unit*, Dequindre Civic Academy, 2016. Collage on inkjet print, 50" × 40".

View of the sports block with the great "deck-solarium".

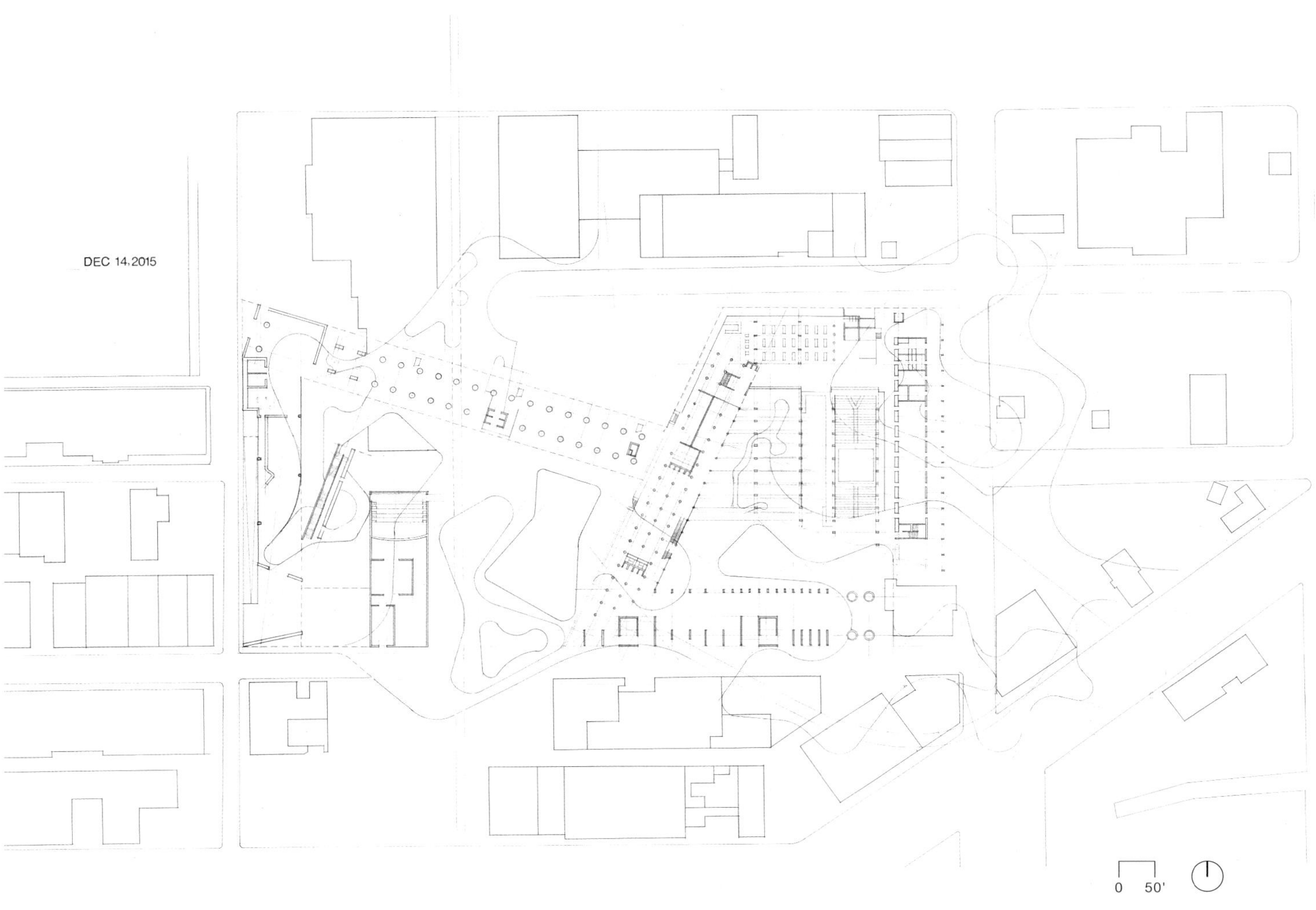

Fig. 32, opposite: This first "sketch" of the project shaped the conceptual development and direction of the DCA by establishing the idea of a large hybrid building, bridging the Dequindre Cut and containing an entire campus within a single building. *Cities within Cities*, Dequindre Civic Academy, 2016. Collage on paper, 8" × 14".

Fig. 33, above: The permeable ground floor creates thresholds between private courtyards, streetscapes, and the Dequindre Cut. The contrasting languages of architecture and landscape overlap and collide to create a richly programmed and complex topography. *Site Plan: Dec. 14, 2015*, Dequindre Civic Academy, 2016. Pencil and transfer letters on vellum, 26" × 36", scale: 1" = 50'.

Fig. 34, above: Interior view of an apartment, floating above the pastures of East Detroit with John Portman's Renaissance Center and downtown Detroit visible in the distance through the porthole window. This collage combines interior views of Le Corbusier's Unité d'Habitation and the National Maritime Union Building in New York with images taken from the site to create an idealized view of domestic life within the DCA. *A Unit of Habitation*, Dequindre Civic Academy, 2016. Collage on paper, 10" × 14".

Fig. 35, opposite: This exterior landscape view manifests the DCA's aspirations to be a eutopian institution dedicated to Detroit's youth. Elements from the architects— Lina Bo Bardi, Le Corbusier, and Enric Miralles and Carme Pinós—are collaged to study the idea of building on the Dequindre Cut. *Enfants Sur Le Paysage*, Dequindre Civic Academy, 2016. Collage on paper, 14" × 20".

Fig. 36: *Toward a Coordinate Unit*, 2016. Collage on paper, 14" x 20".

Walkways interconnect the sports block.

Fig. 37: *A Fortunate Place*,
Dequindre Civic Academy,
2016. Collage on paper,
14" x 20".

Fig. 38, above: *Façade Study*,
Dequindre Civic Academy, 2016.
Ink on tracing paper, 14" x 14".

Fig. 39, opposite: Section model
showing the DCA's school bridge,
which floats over fifty feet above
the Dequindre Cut. The eleven-foot-
high windows within the thick walls
bring in sunlight and provide spectacular views toward and away from
downtown. Skylights penetrating

all three floors allow sunlight
to reach the ground beneath the
bridge. *Section Model Cut Through
the School Bridge*, Dequindre Civic
Academy, 2016. Wood and acrylic,
13 ⅝" × 13" × 12", scale: ⅛" = 1'-0".

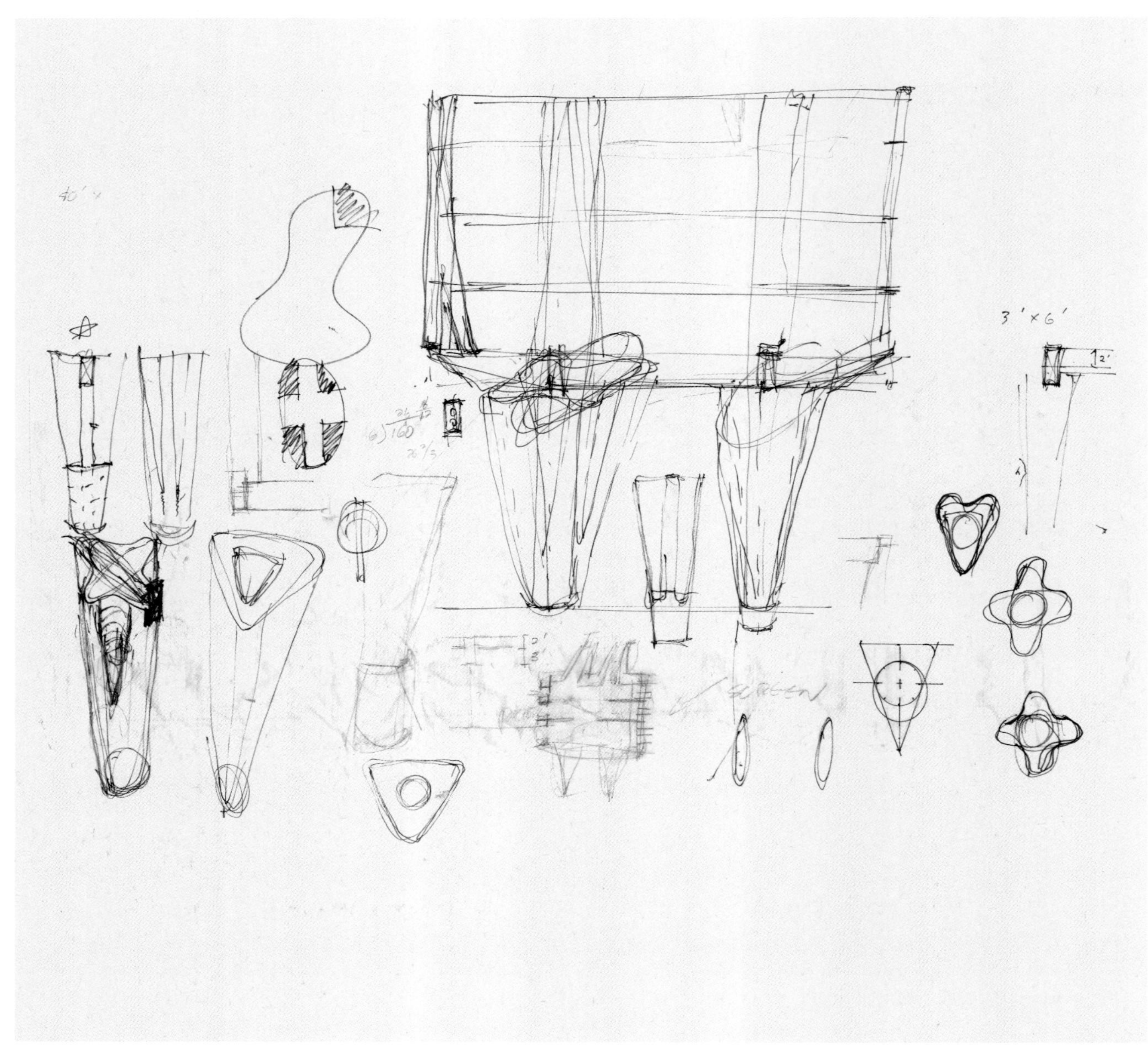

Fig. 40: Sketches created as part of the development of the column supports for the bridge section of the DCA. *Column and Structure Study*, Dequindre Civic Academy, 2016. Ink on tracing paper, 22" x 23".

Fig. 41, left: Cloven column
prototype, 2016. Wood and paint,
scale: 1/8" = 1'-0".

Fig. 42, right: A forest of
monumental cloven columns creates
ceremonial passageways into the
complex from the Dequindre Cut. The
DCA bridge hovers above, penetrated
by a vertical shaft opening to
the sky above. *Section Model Cut
Through the School Bridge*, 2013.
Wood and acrylic, 13 5/8" x 13" x 12".

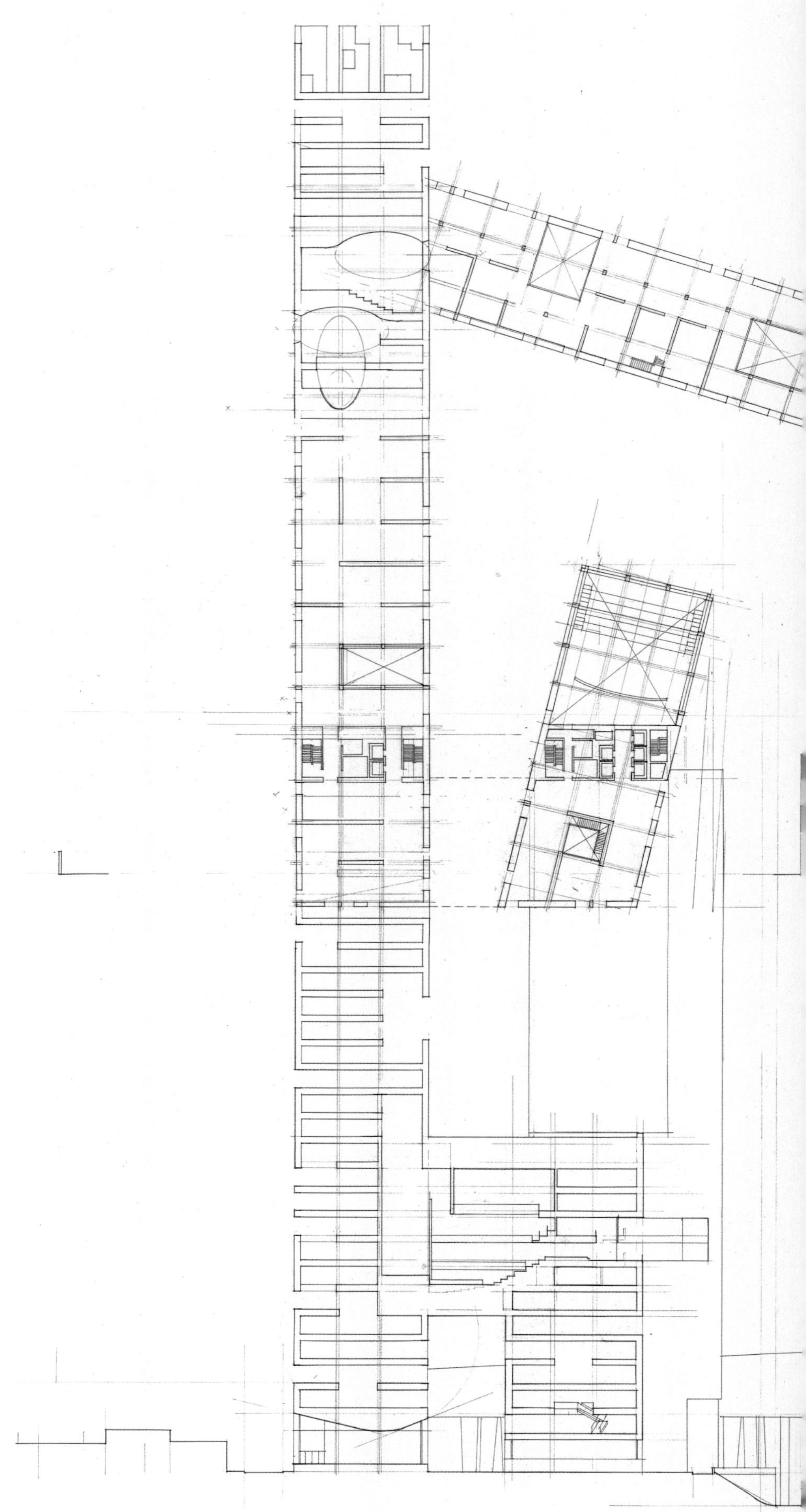

Fig. 43: Each wing embraces a large outdoor patio with strategically placed thresholds that provide security while also creating formal entries to the complex. A third public patio set twenty feet below street level, within the Dequindre Cut, can be accessed via new pedestrian paths and bicycle ramps. A pond for summer swimming and winter skating is the centerpiece of this space, where the school intersects with the public infrastructure of the Dequindre Cut. *Section and Plan Overlay: Feb. 12, 2016, Dequindre Civic Academy, 2016.* Pencil with transfer letters on vellum, 32 ⅜" × 42 ⅛", 1" = 30'.

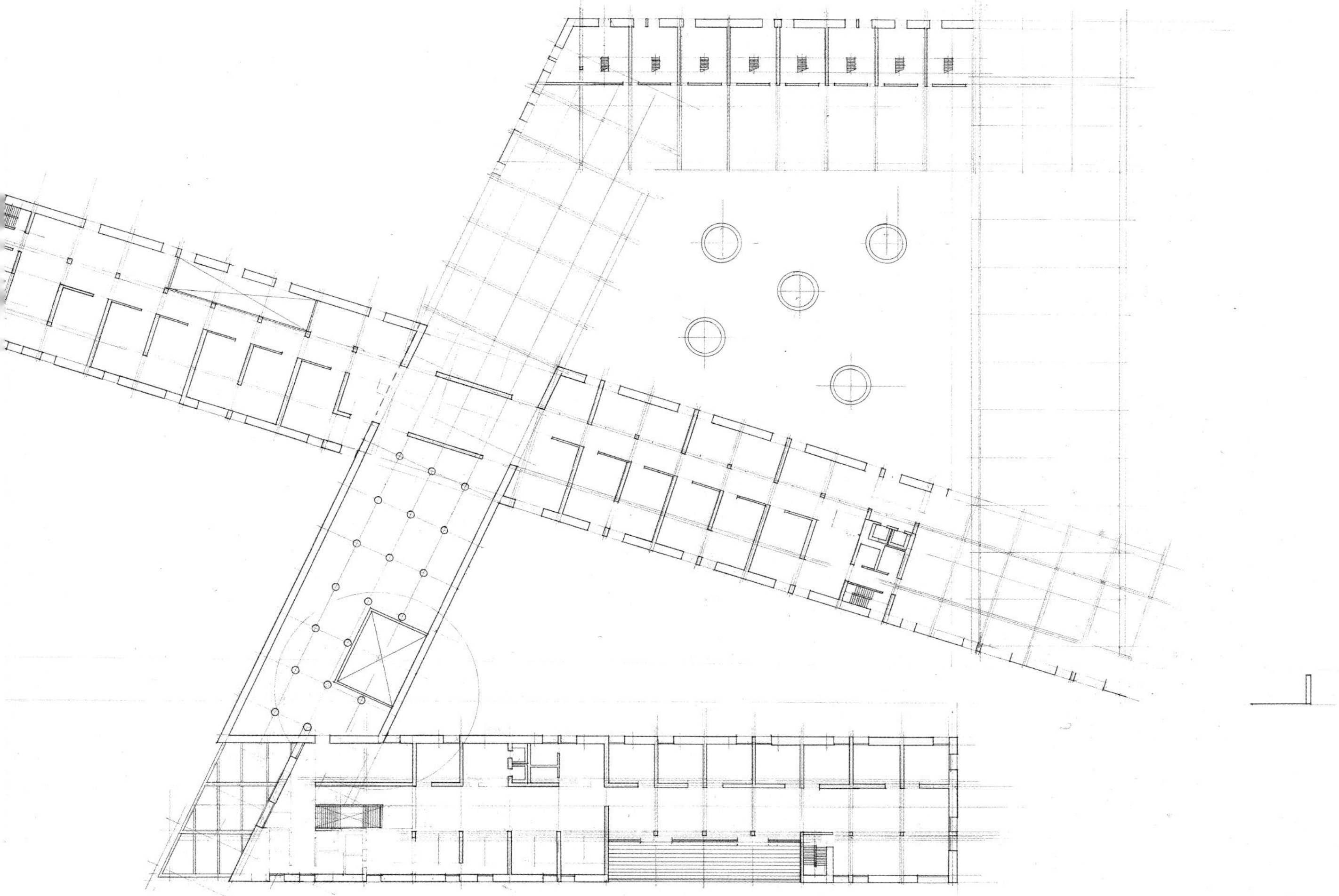

FEB 12, 2016

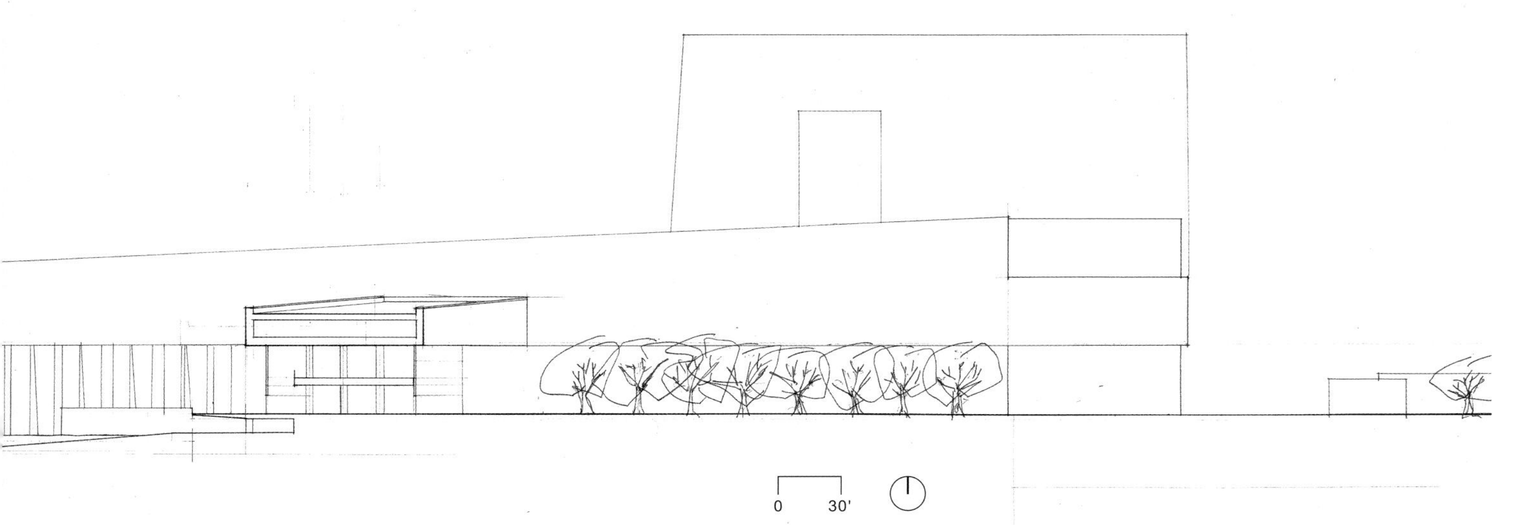

Fig. 44, previous: The vertical west wing contains additional public programs, including cultural spaces, a community college, workshops, and apartments for faculty. The tallest tower measures 865 feet, with a bronze-clad volume housing a worship center near the top and an observatory on the roof. The circular windows in this tower indicate residential dwellings. Model view, Dequindre Civic Academy, 2016. Wood and acrylic, 48 ¾" × 83 ½" × 41 ⅝".

Fig. 45, opposite: DCA is a city within the city. The 2.7-million-square-foot institution is a coordinate unit—a synthetic architectural entity containing many diverse programs and spaces. This all-encompassing institution negotiates the demands of private and public sectors through a new proposal for living. Model, Dequindre Civic Academy, 2016. Wood and acrylic, 48 ¾" × 83 ½" × 41 ⅝".

Like a Creature from Another Time

—

Allison Glenn

It stands out on a highway
Like a creature from another time
It inspires the babies' questions
"What's that?"
For their mothers as they ride
But no one stopped to think about the babies
Or how they would survive
And we've almost lost Detroit
This time
How would we ever get over
Losing our minds?
—*Gil Scott-Heron, lyrics from "We Almost
Lost Detroit" (1977)*

We've almost lost Detroit, this time: Marshall Brown's film *The Dequindre Civic Academy, a Future History* begins on May 21, 2026, near the former site of the Detroit Edison Public School Academy (DEPSA). It describes the fictional origins of his speculative design for a bold future vision requiring a citadel for the care and education of Detroit's children from birth to adulthood. The film's computer-generated voice-over narration and intentional aesthetic set an ominous yet utopian tone, calling to mind Chris Marker's *La Jetée*. Set in a post-apocalyptic society, Marker's film portrays a future Paris after nuclear war, while Brown's film takes place in a future Detroit, sixty years after the partial nuclear meltdown of Fermi 1. Although Scott-Heron's song alludes to the 1967 Detroit Rebellion,[1] it could perhaps also be tied to the ideas that Brown's film brings forth. *The Dequindre Civic Academy* is a film created to position—and arguably to problematize—a corporation's approach to city "revitalization." With still images that, conceptually, frame a window of nonlinear temporality and history, Brown's approach is, on an elemental level, the spatial and temporal domain of postindustrial Detroit—simultaneously

a reverberation of a place in time and an echo of time on a place.

Every time someone reimagines Detroit with good intentions but lack of respect for the city's history, we lose a little bit of what it was. Brown's understanding of the weight and importance of an approach that considers history is immense. Early in the development, Brown asked: What if you could not go outside? What if power was free? What if education was a civic project? What if the children took over? The first collage he created for the Dequindre Civic Academy (DCA), *Cities within Cities* (2016), unites images of SESC Pompéia Lina Bo Bardi's cultural center in São Paolo; Le Corbusier's Unité d'Habitation in Marseilles; and Bertrand Goldberg's mixed-use Marina City in Chicago. Brown's sampling, which the artist calls "stealth collage," is akin to remixing music.[2] The employment of this type of future projecting challenges traditional, purist forms of architecture and design, favoring instead a type of world building that is reliant on already existent structures and forms. How appropriate that Brown's practice of "honorific thievery" be considered for *The Architectural Imagination*, the US Pavilion exhibition at the 2016 Venice Architecture Biennale.[3] Detroit is a city that holds space for radical innovation. It is a landscape onto which many have projected their hopes, dreams, aspirations, and imagined new worlds. It is a well-known urban legend that the Motown staff writer George Clinton and Parliament Funkadelic first launched the Mothership in Detroit's North End or Paradise Valley.[4] Similarly influenced by Bootsy Collins and machination—albeit within the refrain of a postindustrial landscape resulting from the declining automobile industry and subsequent economic divestment in the late twentieth century—Juan Adkins, Derrick May, and Kevin Saunderson began the Detroit techno music revolution while in high school.[5]

Fig. 46, left: Ivan I. Leonidov, The building of the People's Commissariat of Heavy Industry. Competitive project, Round I. Perspective towards the Bolshoi Theater, 1934. Paper, ink, watercolor. 71 ¾" × 46 ¾".

Fig. 47, below: Isamu Noguchi's Philip A. Hart Plaza foregrounds John Portman's Renaissance Center, which rises from downtown Detroit. Photograph of Philip A. Hart Plaza in Detroit, 1972–1979.

Fig. 48, opposite: The drawing reveals a struggle to integrate the contrasting characteristics of architecture and landscape. *Figure/D Ground Study*, Dequindre Civic Academy, 2016. Pencil on vellum, 24" × 30 ⅜", scale: 1" = 50'.

The Belleville Three, as they became known, created a sound that coupled sampling with a four-on-the-floor beat that influenced generations. For these world builders—from Parliament Funkadelic to the Belleville Three—there is a core shared interest in collectivity and a fascination with the possibilities inherent in rethinking existing systems. It is on the shoulders of the incredible ingenuity and experimentation of this city that the design for Brown's Dequindre Civic Academy is built.

Similar to John Portman's coordinate unit—a hybrid structure that houses the diverse programs of a city within a single utopic building—Brown's DCA is also a strategic mash-up of architectural forms and ideas. *Toward a Coordinate Unit* (2016), Brown's large collage, combines fragments of significant late modernist architecture within an homage to *Commisariat of Heavy Industry* (1934), a drawing by the artist, urban planner, and architect Ivan Leonidov.[6] [Fig. 46] The two towers in the collage also recall the twin apartment blocks of Mies van der Rohe's Lafayette Park [Fig. 50], lurking just half a mile down the Dequindre Cut. Brown's multifaceted building is clad in thick walls of a green color called "Cash Money," by the Chicago-based artist Amanda Williams. Deeply inset circular windows generally correspond to housing, and rectangular ones correspond to institutional and administrative programs. And the imposing brutalist complex meets the ground with thick, cloven columns straddling ceremonial pedestrian pathways.

Fig. 49, above: The monumental scale and towers in this aerial view of the DCA stand in stark contrast to the surrounding landscape of East Detroit in the foreground, as it reshapes the skyline of downtown Detroit in the distance. *Citadel, Dequindre Civic Academy*, 2016. Collage on paper, 10 ¼" × 14 ¼".

Fig. 50, left: Lafayette Park by Mies van der Rohe, built in 1956, is a historic urban renewal project in Detroit. The enclave provided inspiration to the DCA as another "city within the city," including not just housing but also a shopping center, school, and other collective facilities. Ludwig Hilberseimer developed the site plan and Alfred Caldwell contributed the landscape design. Mies van der Rohe, Lafayette Park Towers, 2011.

Portman's Renaissance Center opened in the 1970s, a time of divestment in the city. To attract young talent, Ford turned to this visionary architect to represent a new moment for the company. Visions, however, do not always align with their reality. The RenCen's labyrinthine corridors can prove frustrating to navigate, and the respite the building provides from the city suggests that the streets below are not a desirable place. My fondest childhood memory of the RenCen is the fantastical experience of watching the ground drift away while riding the elevators, with their windowed facades, all the way to the top. Elevated, covered tunnels connected pedestrians across busy Jefferson Avenue. The building's inaccessibility at street level suggested a distinction between those inside and outside. As a child, I did not have a sense of the need for a building to provide public space within its walls. I wonder, then, should the children of Detroit require this kind of structure for their future? [Fig. 47]

While Brown's architectural leviathan is definitively Portman-inspired, his extension of the DCA into the surrounding landscape is a bold reconfiguration perhaps illuminated by the work of the artist Isamu Noguchi's groundbreaking designs for Detroit's Philip A. Hart Plaza, a public waterfront park built in 1971.[7] [Fig. 48] Through the development of sublevel plazas that connect the public area around the RenCen to the Detroit Riverfront, Noguchi created an environment of interconnected and programmable gathering spaces. Brown's network of plazas connects the DCA to the existent Dequindre Cut pedestrian byway and Eastern Market neighborhood, resonating with Noguchi's approach. [Fig. 49]

Throughout her history, Detroit has supported new ways of thinking and creating. The innovative legacy that continues to run counter to this city's degradation has kept her going. Approaches to development that disregard the unique fabric of this city, while also discarding the nonlinear temporality to it, will inevitably fail. For those who have dared to imagine her future, the strength lies in the respect for and reuse of existing resources, not the razing of neighborhoods to build community through urban renewal. Perhaps, through the incorporation of Detroit's visionary architectural legacy, Brown's Dequindre Civic Academy will protect Detroit's children from the disavowal of history that new development is typically keen on prioritizing.

NOTES

1 Lyrics to a song penned by Gil Scott-Heron and Brian Jackson, featured on their 1977 collaborative album *Bridges*, released on Arista Records. Although the lyrics point to the Fermi meltdown, it is possible that they reference the rebellion of 1967, the development of the American highway system that decimated communities, the divestment in the city by major corporations moving to the suburbs, and former Mayor Coleman A. Young's tenure as the first Black mayor of the city.

2 Marshall Brown, "MASHUP CITY: Architecture Steals from Contemporary Music," *Believer* 9, no. 6 (2011): 37–38.

3 Twelve teams of American architects were selected to reimagine sites in Detroit as part of *The Architectural Imagination* for the US Pavilion at the 2016 Venice Architecture Biennale. Brown was selected to respond to the site of the Dequindre Cut, a former railroad line turned pedestrian greenway in the Eastern Market neighborhood of Detroit. See The Architectural Imagination, accessed March 21, 2021, http://www.thearchitecturalimagination.org/; and "Marshall Brown: Chimera," Western Exhibitions, accessed March 18, 2021, http://westernexhibitions.com/exhibition/chimera/.

4 Berry Gordy's family was part of the northern exodus brought about by industry and machination. Gordy's founding of Motown Records on the first floor of his home in the Boston-Edison Historic District in 1960 ushered in the Motown sound, and Motown became known for developing talented recording artists with global reach that reigns supreme in the minds of both music aficionados and casual fans alike. See "Berry Gordy," Motown Museum, accessed March 17, 2021, https://www.motownmuseum.org/legacy/berry-gordy/.

5 "The Belleville Three: Techno," Black Music Scholar, accessed March 25, 2021, https://blackmusicscholar.com/the-belleville-three-techno/.

6 "Fall 2020 Lecture Series—Marshall Brown," Carnegie Mellon University, Vimeo, accessed March 18, 2021, https://vimeo.com/467761572.

7 From 1960 to 1990, Noguchi designed civic plazas and playgrounds for cities, many of which remain unrealized. Of the few that came to fruition, one was Noguchi's proposal for Hart Plaza, created in collaboration with Shoji Sadao. Their design was anchored by the Horace E. Dodge Fountain in the center and *Pylon*, a 120-foot torqued stainless steel sculpture at a plaza entrance. See "Noguchi Fountain and Plaza Collection," Isamu Noguchi Archive, accessed March 17, 2021, https://archive.noguchi.org/Browse/archive/facet/collection_facet/id/438.

The New Country

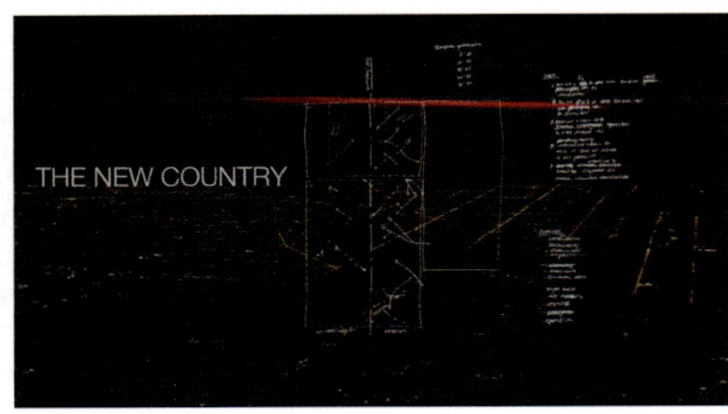

On the South Side of Chicago in 2033,
My father, Daniel Freeman,
Was an architect.
A flood destroyed the city
When he was sixty years old.

For most Chicagoans, their worst fears of
Environmental apocalypse came true.
The ongoing shocks of
Climate mutation provoked an Exodus
To the outskirts of the metropolis.
Two centuries of urban planning,
Engineering, and management
Had failed, disastrously.

Freeman saw changes coming
On the horizon,
And he was prepared.
He and my mother
Stayed on their land.
They lived there
In a house—
A house of Freeman's design.
The house was not large,
But it spread outward
Into the landscape.

They survived
Among a collective.
Citizen settlers.
Back then,
Their neighborhood
Was called Washington Park,
A patch of Chicago

First cultivated
In the nineteenth century,
The vision
Of a Garden City.
Together, Freeman and his people
Finally realized this dream.
Their journey forward
Was also a return;
A Renewal.

The American frontier.
Space,
Time,
Territory.
Unpredictable,
Undetermined,
Unlimited.

So-called nature
Neither conquered,
Nor destroyed.
Freeman's insurgent movement,
Filled the vacuum.
A new way—
Smooth Growth.

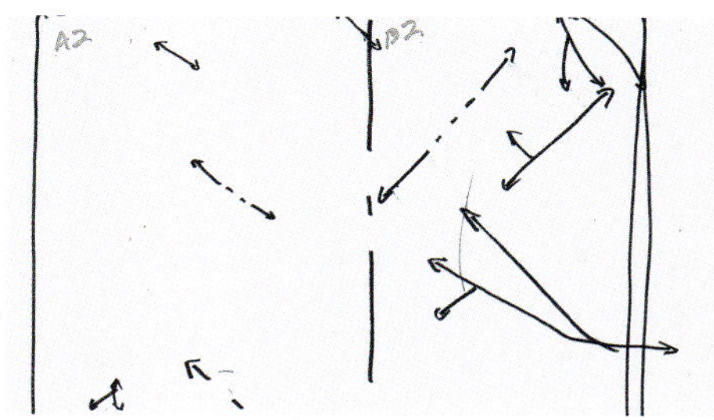 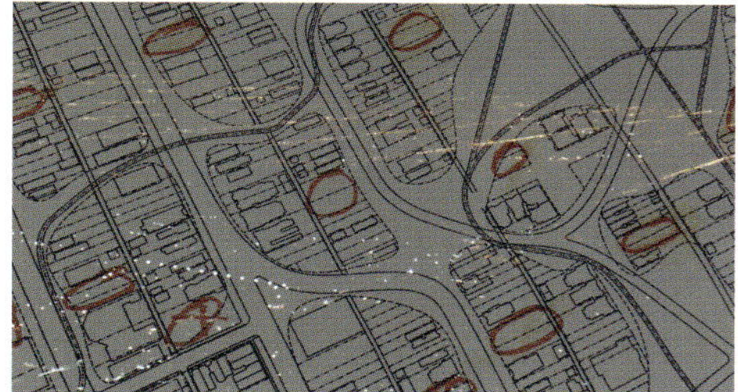 

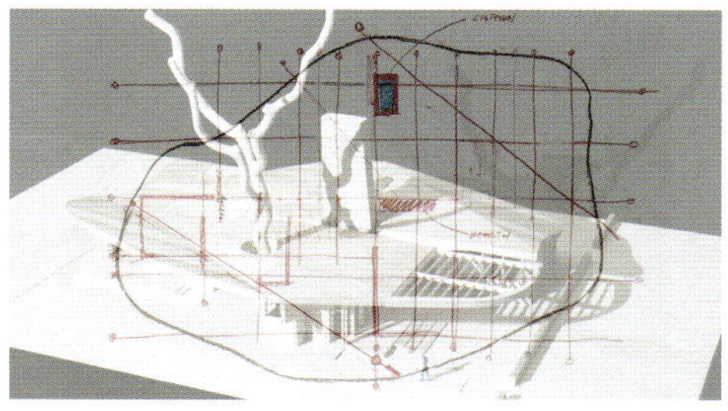  

Citizen settlers
Bundled their resources.
Abandoned spaces were gathered,
And secured through social ownership.
Lawns merged into commons.
Yards burst into broad acres.
They learned to value
Quality over quantity,
Inevitable uncertainty,
And constant change.

Mobility and energy revolutions
Transformed space and time.
Soft infrastructure responded
To emergent flows,
No longer burdened
With false divisions
Between suburbs and downtowns.

Having survived
The fear of shrinking cities,
Freeman's generation found their way
To a new place.
They imagined.
They lived.
They organized
Within principles
Of collective stewardship.

In 2055,
Two years after
Daniel Freeman Passed away.
The Smooth Growth Codes
Were adopted by Cook County, Illinois,
As a new civic charter.

Mine, contributed to ours.
Each, joined the many.
I, surrendered to us.
A truly independent
Society was formed
Through spatial solidarity.

A superorganism,
Its expansions and contractions
Shape and define
A boundless and
Radically American civilization.

This Artificial Eden,
This Middle landscape,
This post-industrial frontier,
Will always be my home.

We call it Territory.
We call it Land.
We call it—
The New Country.

The New Country:
Smooth Growth Urbanism, Chicago

Smooth Growth Urbanism® creates a vision for twenty-first-century garden cities—a hybrid of urban, suburban, and rural spaces. It challenges the dogmatic assumption that growth in new building construction is necessary for urban revitalization. Landscape and infrastructure are used to shape civic space in response to emergent settlement patterns and with the goal of empowering collective neighborhood stewardship. Smooth Growth begins with the recognition that urbanization is an emergent condition—the physical manifestation of collective intelligence over time.[1]

Similar to the decline of many inner-city populations across the United States, Chicago lost two hundred thousand people in the first decade of the twenty-first century. Washington Park is a prototypical neighborhood in this context, positioning it as a first test case for Smooth Growth strategies. After an influx of African Americans during the Great Migration in the early 1900s, Washington Park's population grew dramatically, but since 1970 has dropped over 74 percent, resulting in an abundance of abandoned lots and buildings, akin to other postindustrial cities such as Detroit.

The Smooth Growth Plan for Washington Park responds to a detailed spatial analysis of emergent local conditions. Bundles of private and city-owned properties are gathered into microregions containing every remaining building. The patchwork grid of abandoned properties is reshaped into an archipelago of cohesive, semiprivate territories whose boundaries respond to informal footpaths, driveways, and shortcuts that people have created over time. Ranging from one to ten acres, each subdivision is turned over to residents, who collectively own and improve their shared territory. Former streets remain public rights-of-way and available for planting and recreational uses. Alleys dedicated to private vehicle access incorporate cul-de-sacs used by residents for play and social gathering. A continuous greenway network of remaining land between the microregions is an extension of the Frederick Law Olmsted–designed park on the neighborhood's east side. New roads, walking paths, recreation areas, and wildlife corridors blend civic space and green infrastructure.[2]

Though Smooth Growth is an alternative to infill development, such a revitalized landscape could create the need for a new kind of architecture—the Smooth Growth House. The single-story house takes advantage of abundant land by spreading across a superplot of four combined lots. Unlike a typical townhouse with a formal front, closed sides, and back, the house opens in all directions. The interior is freely shaped on a four-by-four-foot grid and divided between two living clusters, separated by an exterior promenade penetrating the house. A broad and singular timber roof gathers the freely planned interior, thus translating Smooth Growth's urban strategies into architecture.

Smooth Growth addresses depopulation by distinguishing quality from quantity in matters of architecture and urbanism. The Washington Park prototype demonstrates principles and strategies applicable to many American cities in need of innovative approaches to development at moderate or lower densities. From neighborhood to house, Smooth Growth is a landscape of cooperative independence. It projects a flexible geography for shifting settlement patterns and consequently reasserts the value of open land in cities—a vision for a dynamic hybrid landscape combining the best aspects of urban, suburban, and rural life.

NOTES

1   For more on the theory of emergent systems, see Steven Johnson, *Emergence: The Connected Lives of Ants, Brains, Cities, and Software* (New York: Scribner, 2001). Johnson uses the relatively new field of emergence studies in the sciences to explain how cities grow in many ways similar to nondirected systems found in nature such as ant colonies and other superorganisms. The theory is based on the collective intelligence manifested by large numbers of simple agents working together over time.

2   Olmsted and his partner, Calvert Vaux, began the design for Washington Park in 1870. The park's blueprints were burned in the Great Chicago Fire of 1871; however, Horace William Shaler Cleveland completed the work, largely capturing Olmstead and Vaux's original design.

Fig. 51: The large-scale model that Brown created to show the Smooth Growth Plan for Washington Park recalls Frank Lloyd Wright's model of Broadacre City. This scale emphasizes the vastness of the American landscape and the potential for the plan to expand out with the Jeffersonian grid. The polychromatic color scheme illustrates the reorganization of the neighborhood into a series of semi-independent microregions formed through collective negotiation. The model was designed to be immersive, engaging, and changeable over time. Marshall Brown and the Smooth Growth Model for Washington Park, Smooth Growth, 2013. Mixed media, 12' × 14'.

Fig. 52, opposite: Detail of the Smooth Growth model in its early stages showing existing houses consolidated into microregions. The stripes and crosses indicate former streets that will remain public right-of-ways where landscape improvements and recreation can occur. These traces of the grid represent the history of the site and emphasize that Smooth Growth is an overlay onto the existing urban fabric rather than a tabula rasa approach to urbanism. Model Detail of Microregions, Smooth Growth, 2012. Mixed media.

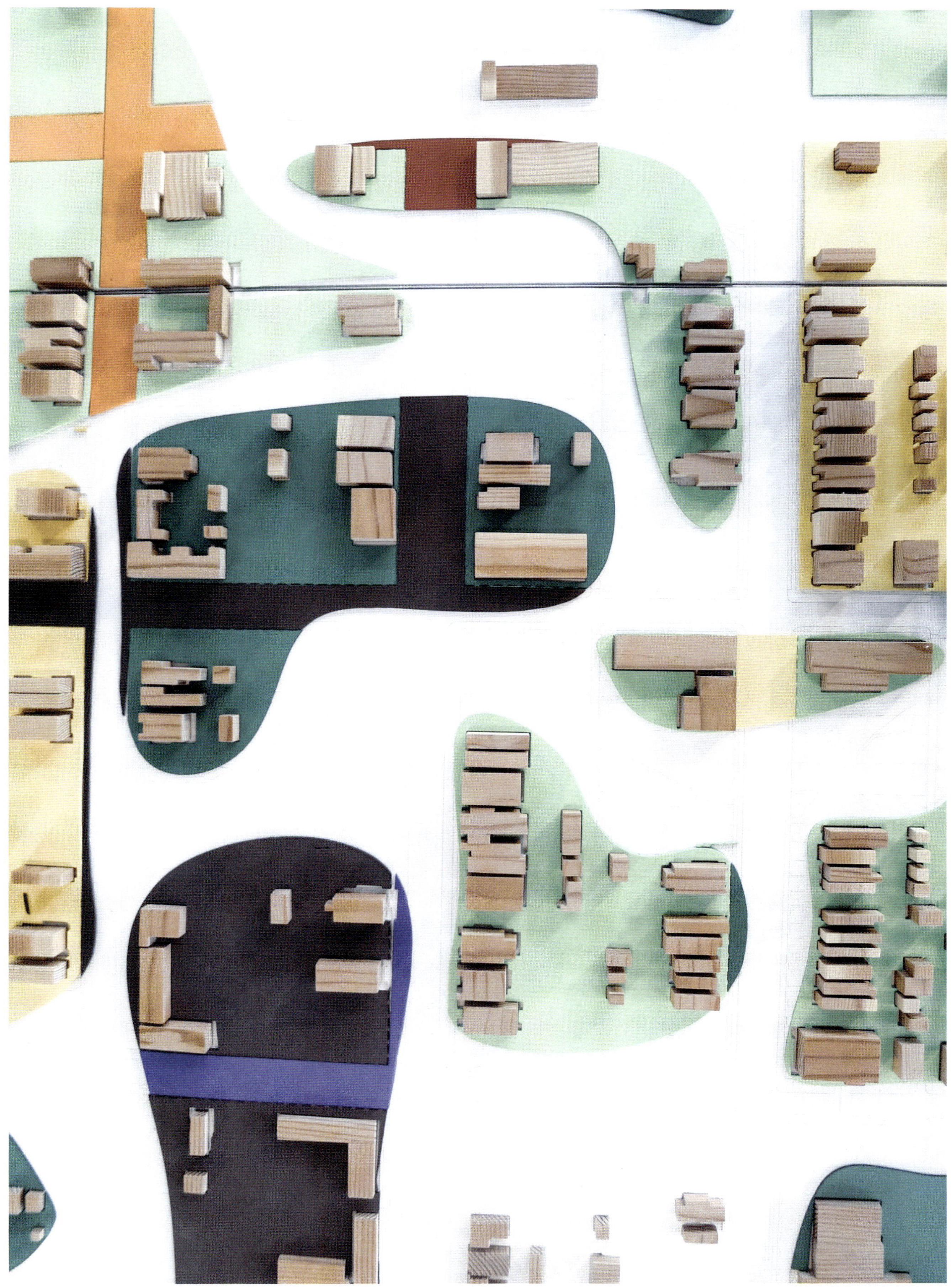

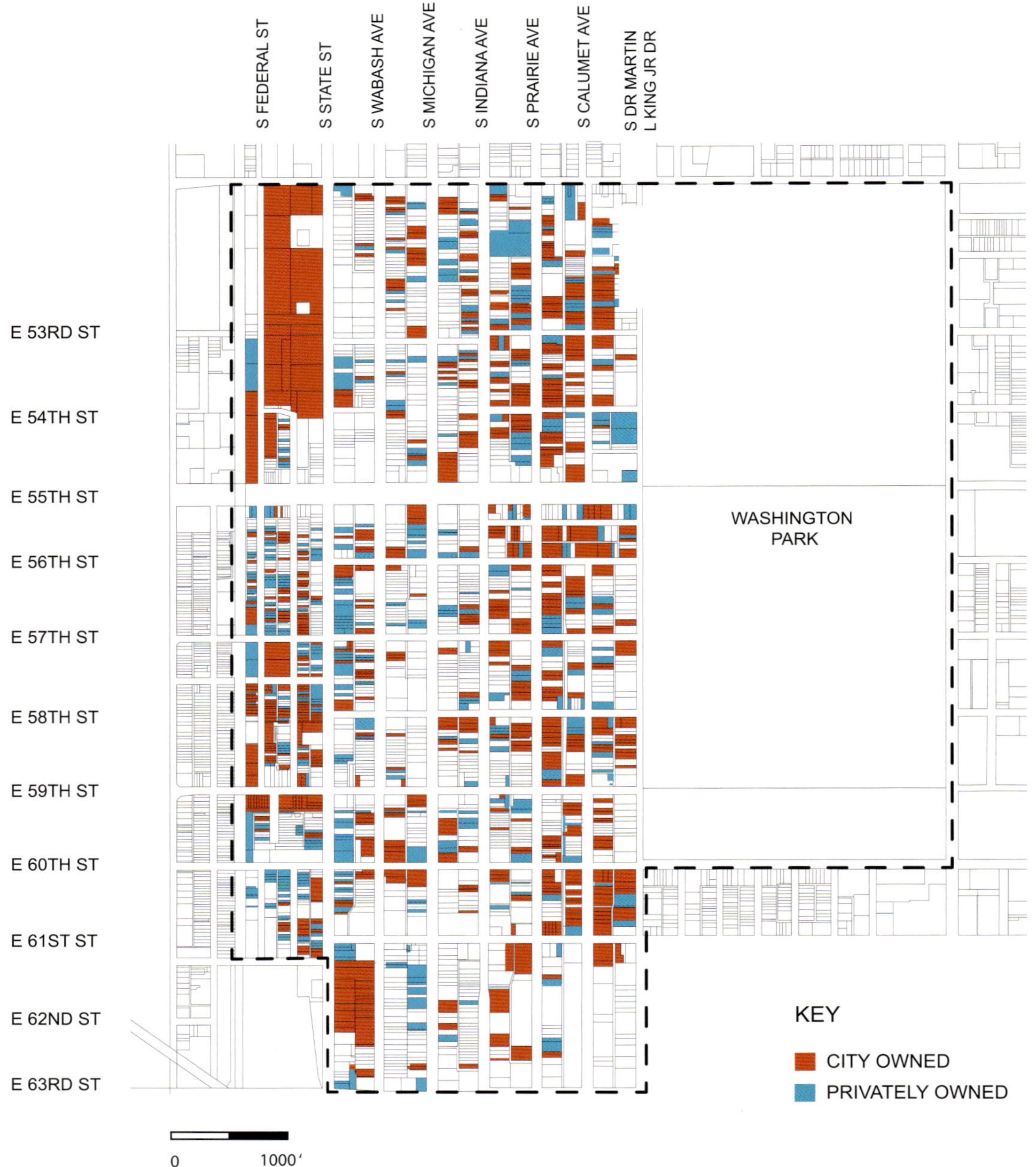

Fig. 53: The total amount of available land in Washington Park (red and blue parcels) is approximately 6.6 million square feet. Of the available land in Washington Park 65.5 percent is owned by the City of Chicago together with the Chicago Housing Authority (red parcels). The remaining 34.5 percent is distributed among private owners (blue parcels).

The city-owned parcels represent a total of 4.32 million square feet (99 acres), or 22.9 percent of the total developable land in the neighborhood. This is an area the size of approximately four Millennium Parks. Available Land Ownership, 2012. Digital diagram.

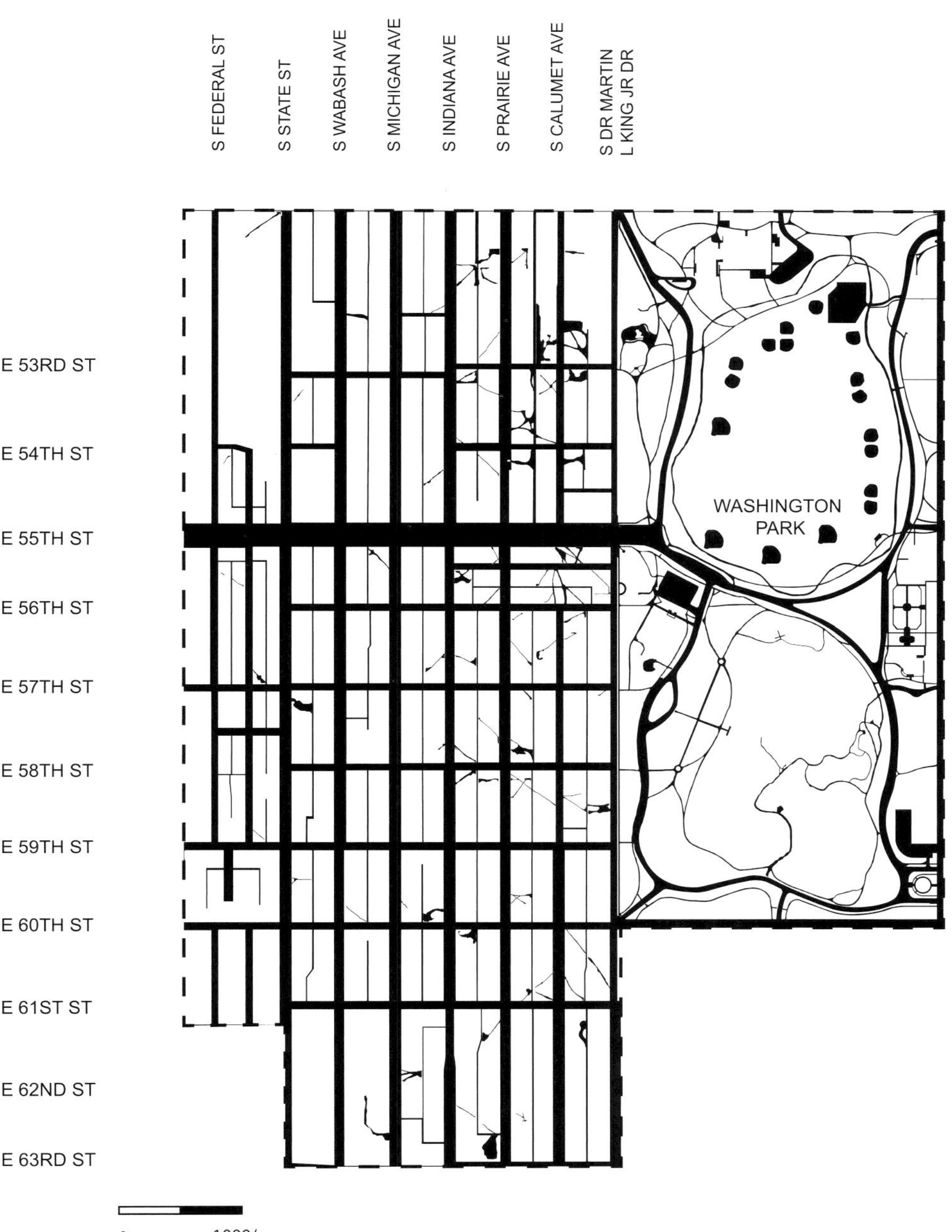

Fig. 54: Shortcuts repeated by pedestrians and vehicles have carved an informal, alternative circulation network into the landscape of Washington Park. These desire lines are the physical manifestation of a collective intelligence that could serve as the basis for the neighborhood's new structure. Grid Evolution, 2012. Digital diagram.

Fig. 55, following page: Close-up view of the Smooth Growth model, showing the effects of bundling all of the existing buildings into cohesive territories. The bands signify street spaces captured within the superplots that will remain semi-public rights of way. Smooth Growth House model, 2019. Wood and acrylic, 11" x 42" x 25", scale: 1/4" = 1'-0".

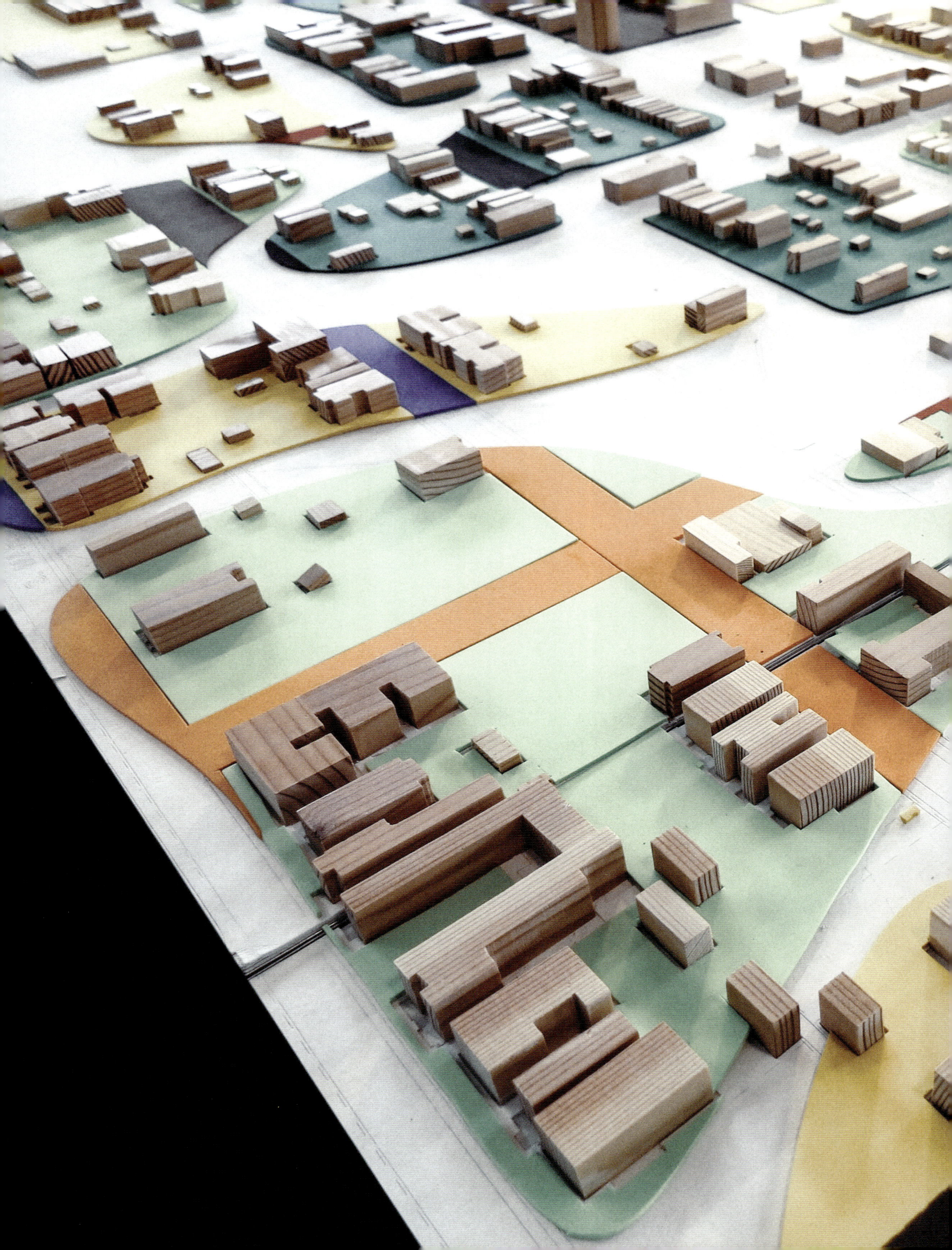

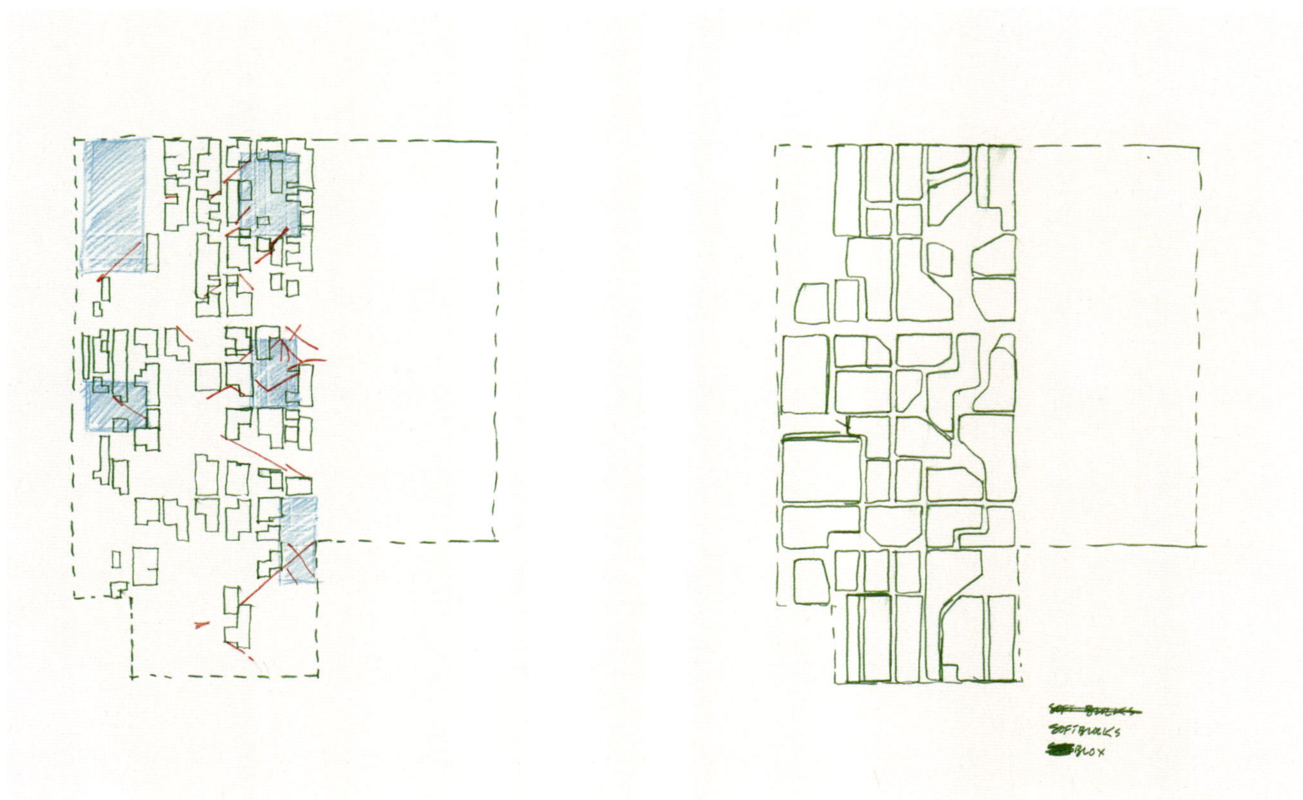

Figs. 56, 57, and 58, above and
opposite: A series of sketches used to
show the replanning of Washington Park
with existing housing clusters bundled
together in green and the pedestrian
shortcuts demarcated in red. The existing
homes alongside the informal routes
of circulation merge to create an ordered
yet organic plan. *Archipelago Number One*,
Smooth Growth, 2012. Marker on tracing
paper, 23" x 17 ¾"; *Archipelago Number
Two*, Smooth Growth, 2012. Marker on
tracing paper, 24" x 17 ¾"; *Archipelago
Number Three*, Smooth Growth, 2012.
Marker on tracing paper, 20" x 24".

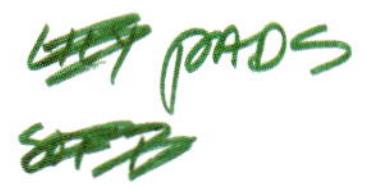
LILY PADS
SEED

COHERENCE
IS
THE PROBLEM.

Fig. 59: Every remaining building in Washington Park is bundled together within a superplot, each collectively owned and maintained by its residents. The residual land becomes a cohesive space for constructing a revitalized civic realm, connected to and extending from the park. Red marks signify existing pedestrian shortcuts, which are used to guide the creation of new circulation patterns. Smooth Growth Plan for Washington Park, 2013. Digital diagram.

Fig. 60: Smooth Growth Urbanism is a progressive model for city building that moves beyond false divisions between urban and suburban, city and country. Smooth Growth uses landscape, infrastructure, and civic space to rebuild neighborhoods. It is a project that engages cities as emergent systems—physical manifestations of human collective intelligence. Smooth Growth is not a tabula rasa scheme that remakes the world from scratch. Public and private landscapes are no longer in conflict but fluidly woven together to create a twenty-first-century garden city. Smooth Growth Plan for Washington Park, Smooth Growth, 2012. Digital map.

Fig. 61: The Smooth Growth House
is situated within a typical block
in this sketch. It indicates how
the existing alley augmented with
cul-de-sacs provides vehicle access
at the top of the drawing and the
former street on the bottom converted
to a pedestrian promenade. Four
contiguous lots are combined to
create a superplot—a single property
now nearly square in its proportions
and about one quarter of an acre,
framed by existing houses on the right
and left of the sketch. Smooth Growth
House Landscape Study, Smooth Growth,
2019. Ink and Prismacolor on layered
tracing paper, 25" × 27".

Fig. 62: View of the Smooth Growth
House showing the carport and
breezeway, which separate the two
portions of the house. A stair rises
along the chimney, providing views
out onto the landscape. Smooth Growth
House model, 2019. Wood and acrylic,
11" x 42" x 25", scale: 1/4" = 1'-0".

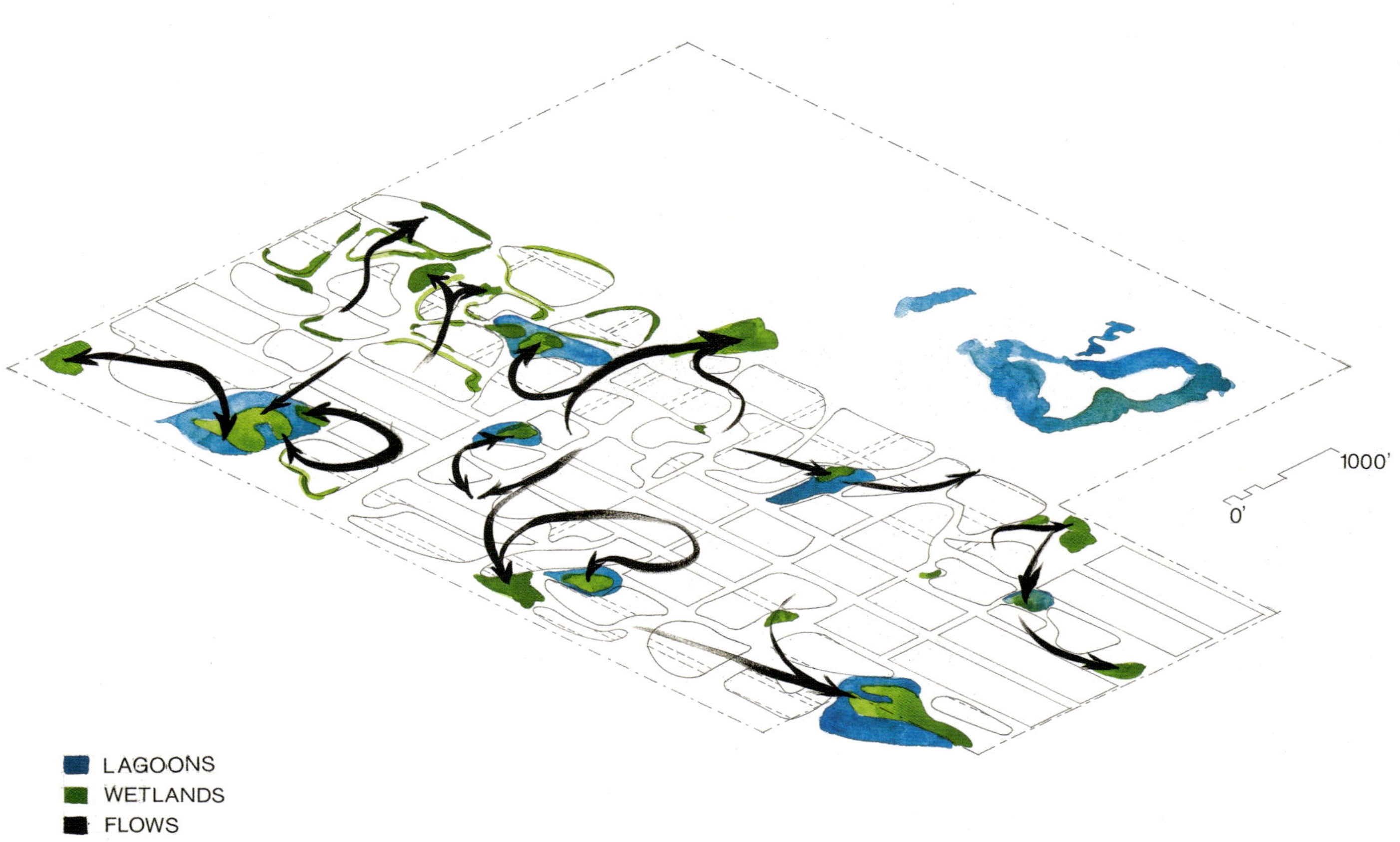

Fig. 63: Axonometric diagram studying the flow of water in the new Washington Park. Wetlands and lagoons are strategically placed to absorb stormwater on site. *Hydrology Study*, Smooth Growth Plan for Washington Park, 2020. Pencil and gouache on paper, 18" x 24".

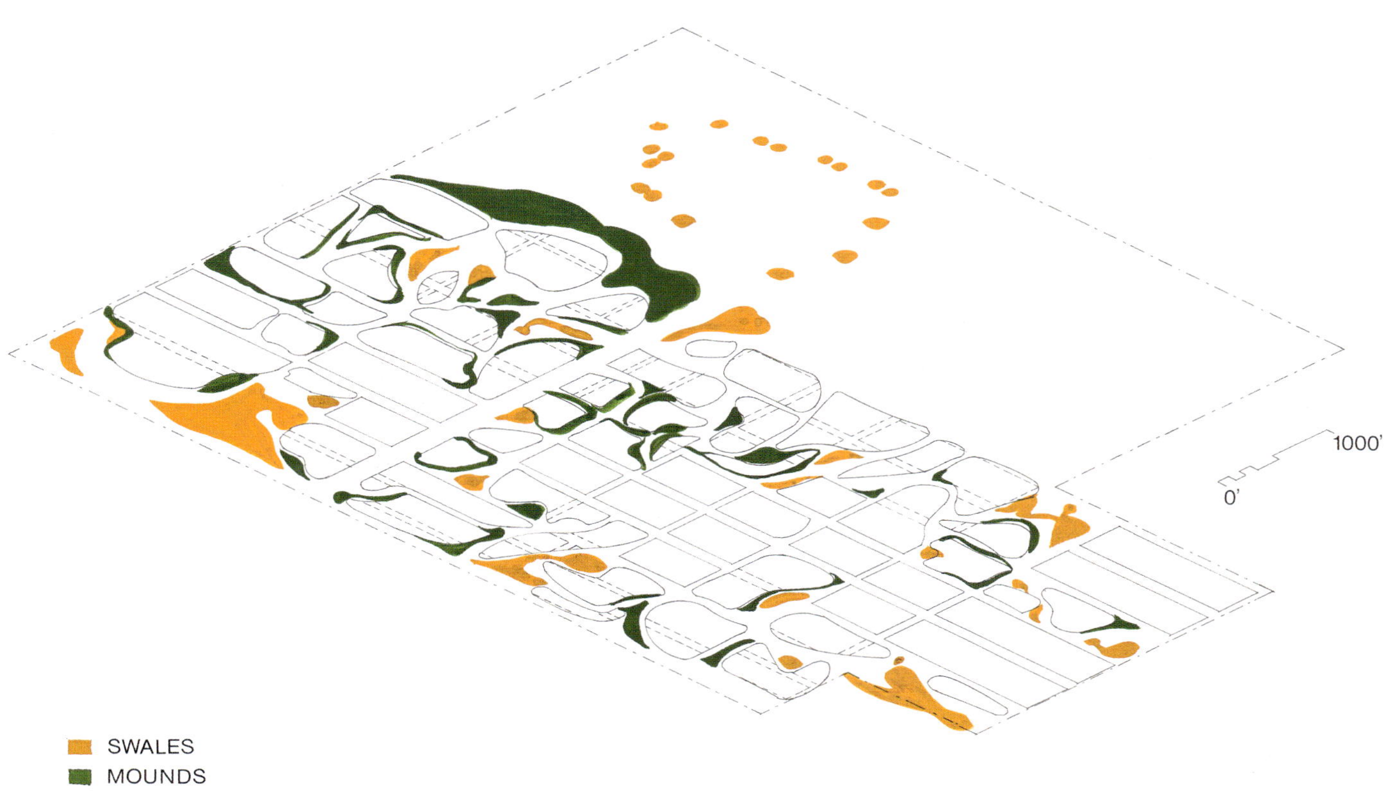

Fig. 64, above: Axonometric diagram studying topography in the new Washington Park. Cut and fill operations are introduced to create mounds and swales that respond to the new urban structure, provide spatial variation, and support ecological objectives such as water flow and containment. *Topography Study*, Smooth Growth Plan for Washington Park, 2020. Pencil and gouache on paper, 18" x 24".

Fig. 65, overleaf: This elevation view of the Smooth Growth House shows how the interior spaces open onto the landscape and are sheltered by the overhanging roof. The roof is penetrated by the hearth and a large tree, demonstrating the integration of natural and domestic landscapes. Smooth Growth House model, 2019. Wood and acrylic, 11" x 42" x 25", scale: 1/4" = 1'-0".

BB
2×12" rafters
+ 13'-6"
+ 10'
2'
AA

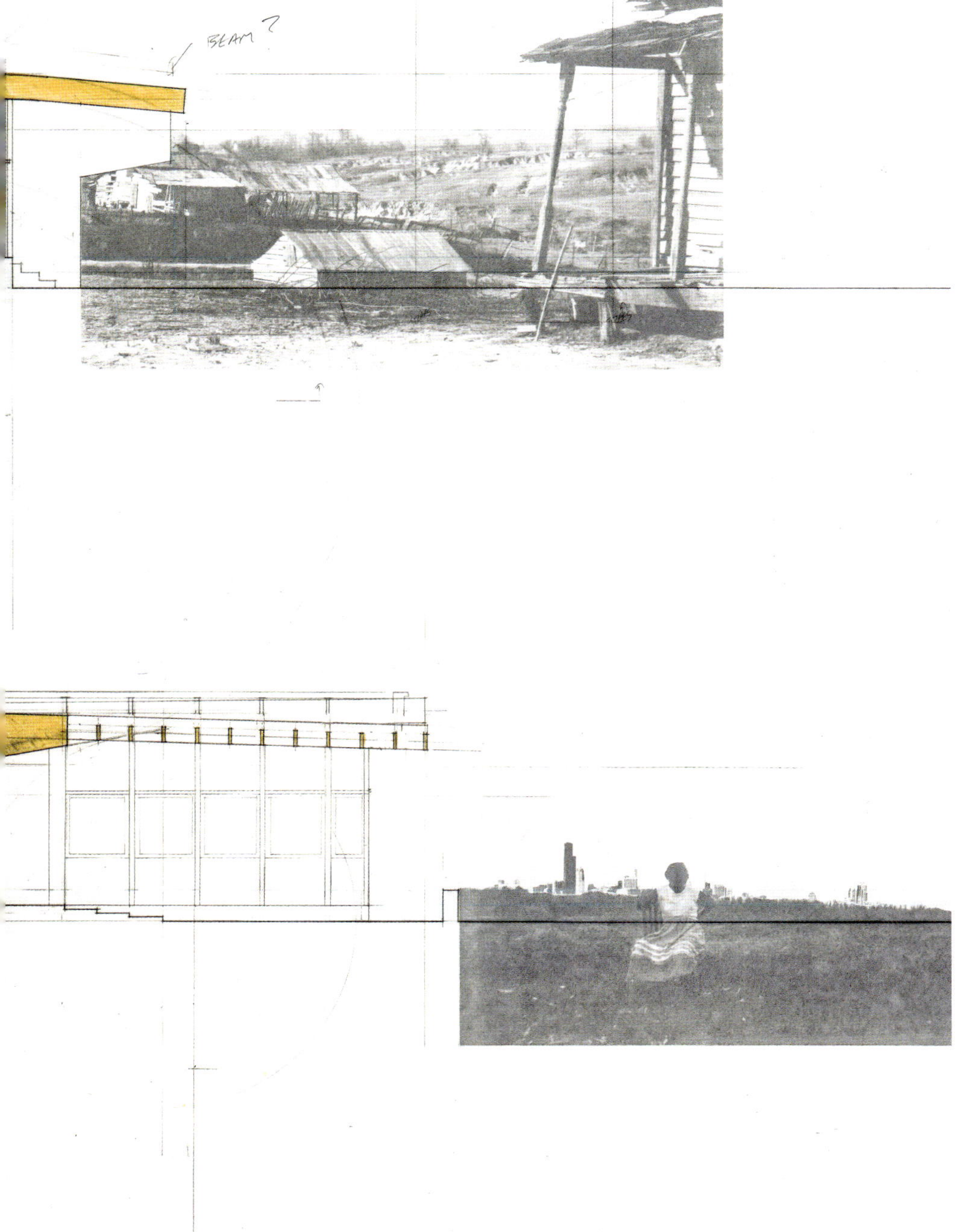

Fig. 66: Smooth Growth House's form responds to the simultaneous realities of domestic life and the urban environment. The upper surface is strategically folded to climb up and capture light while providing shade and intimacy where necessary. The curvaceous ceiling is a landscape that creates a rhythm of vertical expansion and compression as it moves from outside to inside and outside again. *A New Place*, Smooth Growth, 2019. Collage with pencil, Prismacolor, and Letraset on drafting film, 32" × 41 ¾".

Fig. 67: Individual spaces are freely shaped as semi-independent volumes and distributed between two living clusters, separated by an exterior walkway. Similar to the microregions superimposed onto Chicago's grid, the Cartesian fragments of the house are gathered beneath the single curvilinear form of the roof. *Plan for an American House*, Smooth Growth, 2019. Pencil and Prismacolor on drafting film, 34 ½" × 43".

A
B
B
A
0   4ft

Fig. 68, opposite: Working drawing used to translate between the spatial promise of the sections and the formal reality of the built model. Each profile became a template for cutting, shaping, and assembling the roof form. *Chora (the fold and the wave)*, Smooth Growth, 2019. Pencil on drafting film, 32" × 37 ⅜".

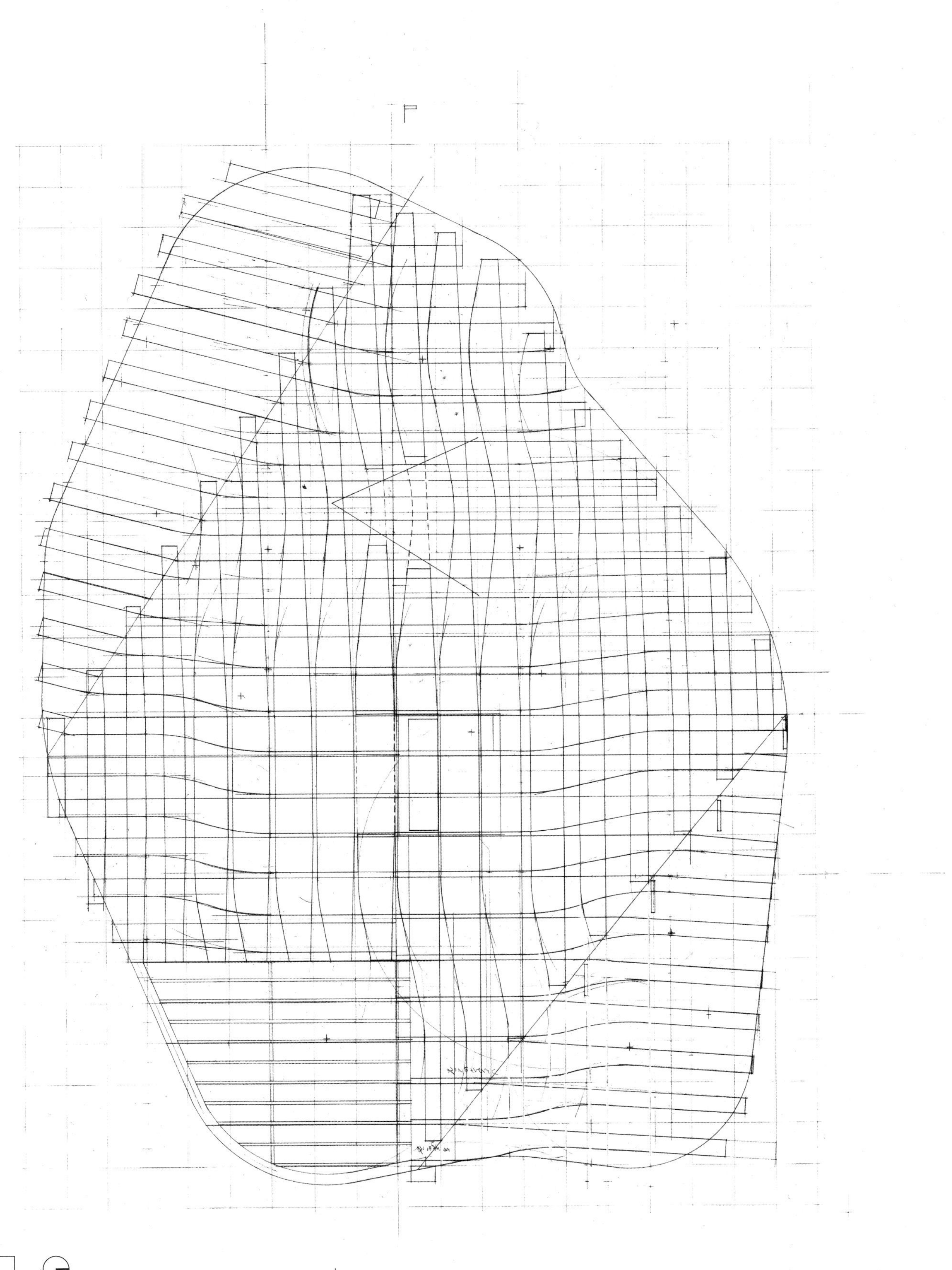

0   4ft

Fig. 69: Smooth Growth House model
roof underbelly, in progress, 2019.
Wood. Scale: ¼" – 1'-0".

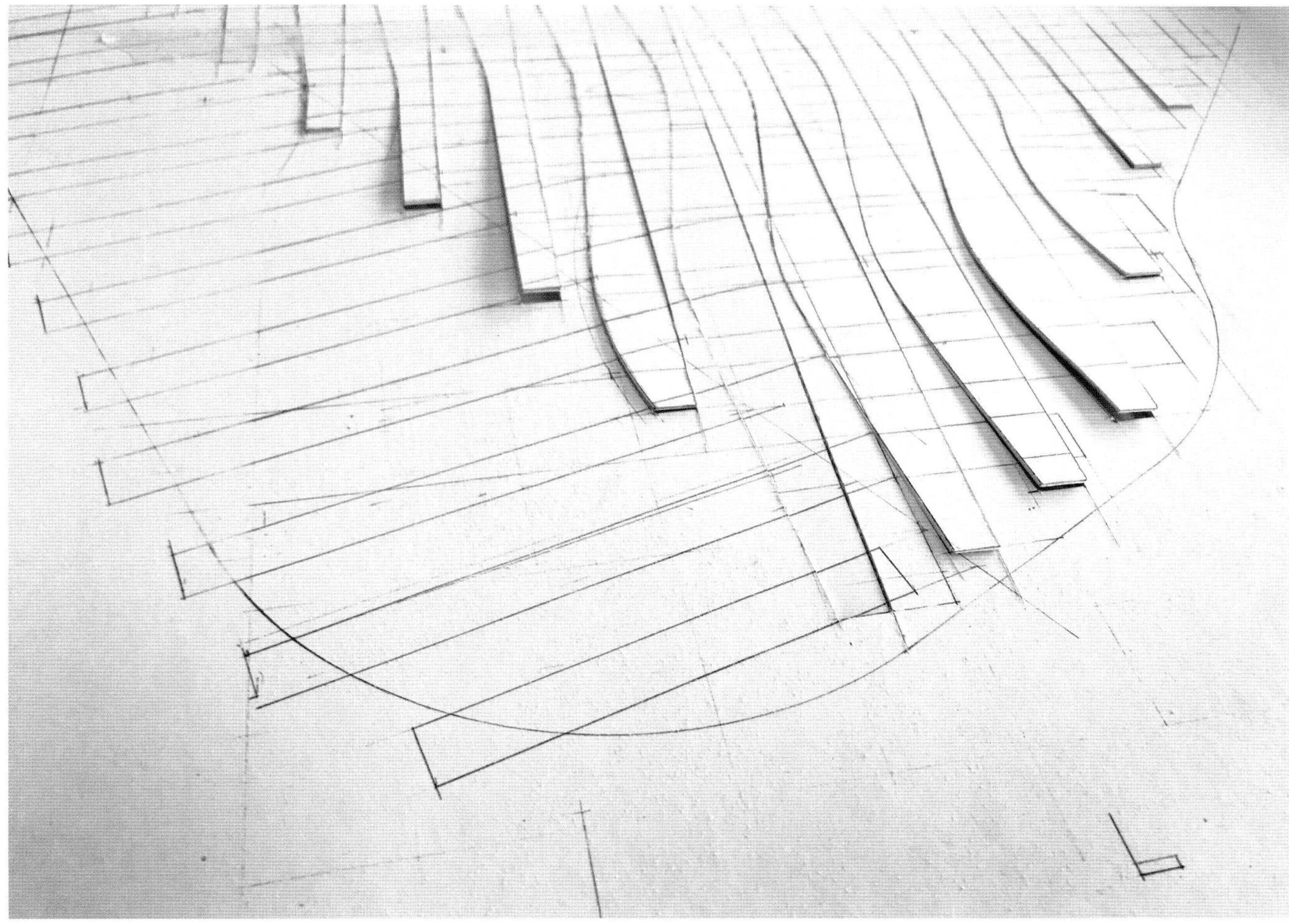

Fig. 70: Smooth Growth House roof
templates, 2019. Inkjet print on paper
and chipboard. Scale: ¼" – 1'-0".

Fig. 71, opposite: This exploded oblique drawing dissects the Smooth Growth House into four layers from top to bottom. The ground plane articulates the subtle transitions between different uses. Springing out from the hearth, interior partitions loosely define more private spaces within the house. Wood and glass enclosures provide ample views and access to the landscape. And the roof, shown here in worm's-eye view, shades and brings cohesion to the house as a whole. *Elements of an American House*, Smooth Growth, 2019. Pencil and Prismacolor on drafting film, 74" × 32".

Fig. 72, overleaf: Viewed from above, the Smooth Growth House does not have a front or back, but engages the landscape in 360 degrees. The roof becomes a second landscape that is penetrated by the juxtaposed figures of the hearth and a tree. Model, Smooth Growth House, 2019. Wood and acrylic, 11" × 42" × 25", scale: ¼" = 1'-0".

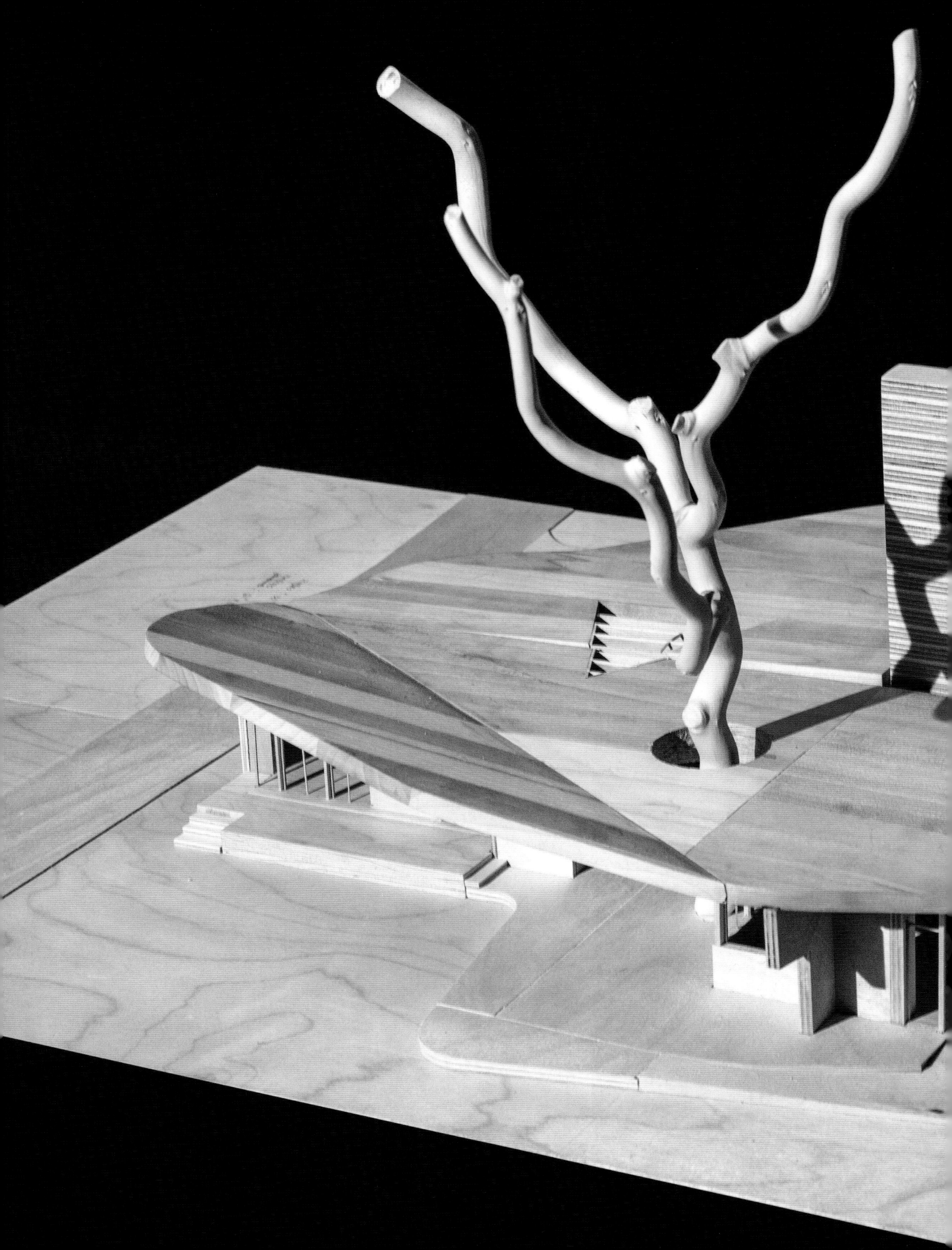

The New Old Frontier

—

Adrienne Brown

Can we understand open lots in urban neighborhoods that have experienced significant population loss as a mode of presence rather than a symptom of failure? As a map for a more collective future rooted in cooperative forms of sovereignty rather than an index of decline in need of extensive and expensive repair? This is the provocation of Marshall Brown's Smooth Growth Urbanism®, a concept that builds on previous theorizations of garden cities as well as the ongoing life of Chicago's Washington Park community that, despite having lost a substantial number of residents over several decades, continues on as an urban community. What happens when urbanists privilege creatively capturing what remains in and of a place rather than redeveloping for future growth that, as history shows, often comes at the expense of those who stay the residential course?

If we are not quite ready yet for Smooth Growth's vision of collective stewardship through social ownership, Brown imagines we are merely one cosmic climate event away from leaping into this new reality. Nothing short of catastrophe, it seems, could foster the mass relinquishing of massive redevelopment as the magic elixir for urbanism. In the mythos later invented to accompany the Smooth Growth project, Brown ascribes this vision for Washington Park to Daniel Freeman—a fictional architect who, after a 2033 flood devastates Chicago, imagines a new way for his community of citizen settlers to realize the dream of garden city living in the wake of sudden ecological disaster preceded by a slower process of population loss.[1] By bundling the neighborhood's remaining resources into microregions of clustered occupied properties to be governed by small collectives of occupants, Smooth Growth approaches abandonment as an opportunity to imagine new forms of sovereignty embedded in the landscape of the present. Open lots, improvised shortcuts, and old boulevards become the materials for conceptualizing new territorial forms of governance, maintenance, and care in the name of stabilization rather than expansion.

In Brown's narrative, Daniel Freeman is sixty years old at the time of the Great Flood. Presuming Freeman was a long-term resident of Washington Park, he would have lived through the longer arc of population loss and disinvestment in his community preceding the city's broader ecological dismantling. Whereas Washington Park was home to more than forty-six thousand residents in 1970, by 2018, that number had shrunk to eleven thousand.[2] This demographic change registers within the landscape via underutilized land lots, but the neighborhood also hosts public art, tended homes and lots, and community gardens—sites connected to one another through improvised shortcuts that inscribe emerging patterns of use. [Fig. 74] Given the embrace of collage across Brown's projects, we might consider his approach in Smooth Growth as an extension of this ethos, collecting and bundling the patterns, paths, and lots already existing in Washington Park to help us better see the function of what was there all along. As Brown suggests and Freeman infers, Washington Park is not a tabula rasa—not now and not in 2033. Freeman's experience of living through the push and pull of retraction and remaking, of demographic and infrastructural transformation facilitating new habits of occupation and perception, equipped him to arrive at his postapocalyptic plan just as much as formal histories of architecture and urbanism. Unlike the massive remaking of the city in the wake of the Great Chicago Fire of 1871, the 2033 flood becomes an occasion for reorganizing urban living to reflect the history of its use rather than reimagining the form of the city from scratch. Freeman reimagines the frontier future of Chicago

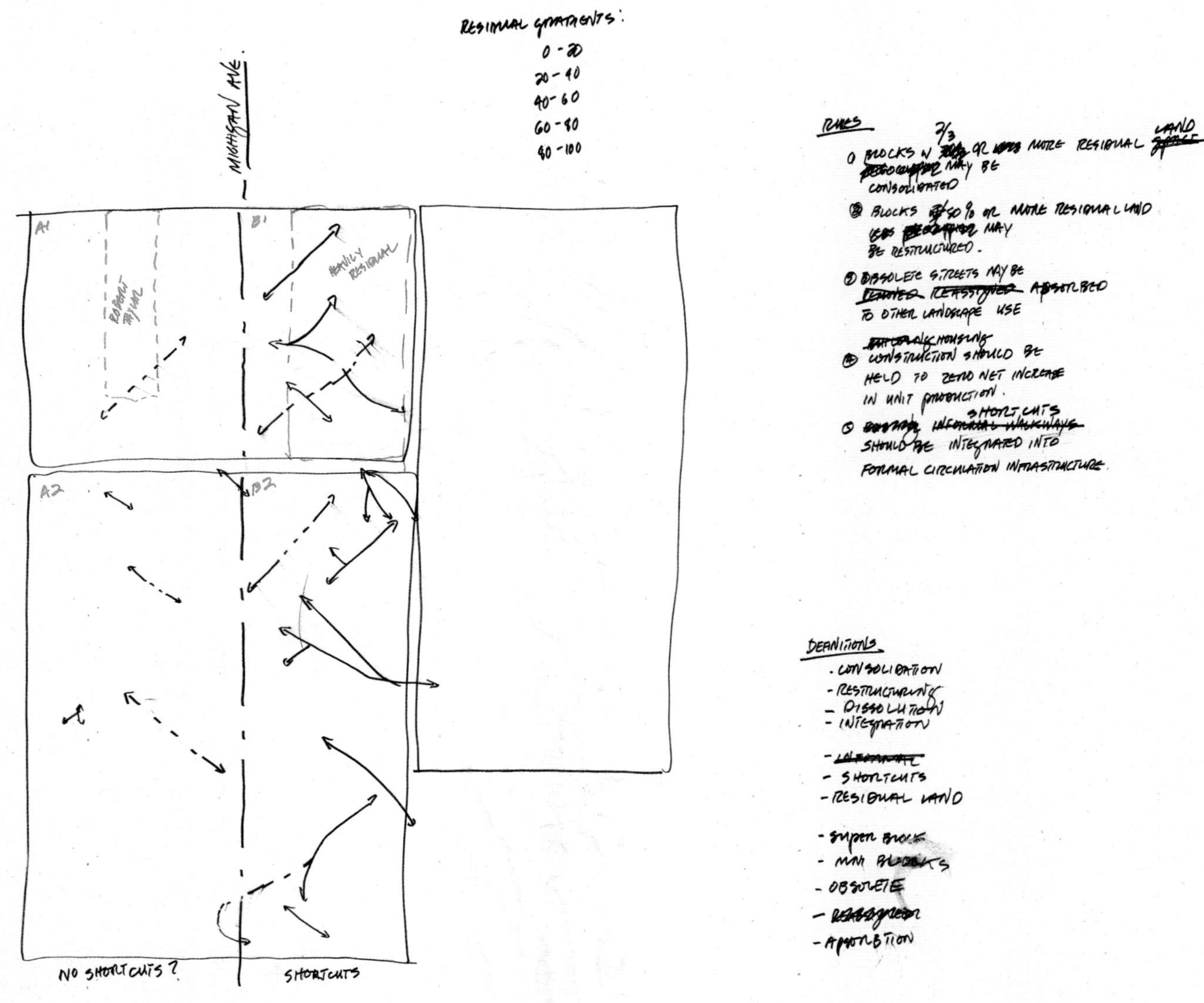

Fig. 73: This sketch demonstrates a set of principles that constitute Smooth Growth and address the mismatch between the nineteenth-century urban structure and twenty-first-century settlement patterns. The structure of Smooth Growth focuses on the reconfiguration of blocks, landscape, and infrastructure in the absence of population growth, establishing a practical yet optimistic approach to urban revitalization for cities across America. *Entropy, Rules, Definitions*, Smooth Growth, 2012. Marker on tracing paper, 23 ¾" × 25 ½".

Fig. 74, left: Washington Park has experienced dramatic population decline since the 1970s, leaving the formerly densely packed neighborhood full of open lots and abandoned properties. Aerial View of Washington Park, ca. 2012.

Fig. 75, right: A distant view toward Chicago's Robert Taylor Homes housing project in the early stages of demolition. A crane can be seen left of the housing block, center frame. Camilo José Vergara, View along S. Dearborn Street towards E. 54th St., Chicago, November 2000.

rooted in an ethos of survival that is not predicated on scorched-earth settler colonialism but collective management in tune with occupation patterns of the past and present.

While population shifts have dominated the civic discourse about Washington Park over the past few decades, the neighborhood has perennially existed just outside or beyond more-heralded parts of Chicago's South Side such as Bronzeville and Hyde Park. Even the neighborhood's best-known cultural claim to fame—as the local inspiration behind the blockbuster midcentury play *A Raisin in the Sun*—manages to just shirk Washington Park proper.[3] Further overshadowing the neighborhood's status as a neighborhood are the two large green spaces along its longitudinal boundaries. [Fig. 74] The first is the neighborhood's namesake—the 372-acre Washington Park designed by Frederick Law Olmsted and Calvert Vaux and completed in the early 1870s.[4] Host to large, sprawling lawns and a series of scenic lagoons, this bucolic park was also a site of intense racial violence in the early twentieth century, as African Americans increasingly insisted on their right to this civic amenity.[5] In addition to this large park just east of the neighborhood, the 2007 demolition of the Robert Taylor Homes, stretching across the western part of Washington Park and the Grand Boulevard neighborhood to the north, added another large swath of open space to its footprint. [Fig. 75] The largest public housing development in the country when it was built, the Robert Taylor development housed as many as twenty-seven thousand people at its peak.[6] Since its destruction, which was opposed by the majority of its residents at the time, the land on which it stood has

Fig. 76: View of the large-scale model for Broadacre City with Frank Lloyd Wright in the distance. In a depiction of the Smooth Growth model, Brown references this image by the insertion of himself—the author—in a similar fashion to Wright. Frank Lloyd Wright with his Broadacre City model, 1935.

reverted to flat green lawn, awaiting much promised redevelopment.

There is a certain irony to the fact that the histories of these two canonical projects of civic planning, Olmsted's Washington Park and the Robert Taylor Homes—each of which aspired and failed in different ways to function as beacons of a democratic spirit rooted in equity—have not dampened the general belief that large-scale redevelopment remains the magic bullet for Washington Park's ailments. But even as massive and pricey projects endure as mythic white whales of desirable growth, Brown attends to the overlooked and understudied residential practices of those who have lived in and amid these two models of urbanism, and finds within these more everyday practices and patterns a different and more sustainable model of city living.

Given Washington Park's status as an urban community defined by sizeable green spaces to the east and west with many unoccupied lots in between, it follows that Smooth Growth would also take inspiration from Frank Lloyd Wright's Broadacre City, organized around a similar commitment to low density and decentralization. Like Freeman's plan in the wake of a major flood, Wright, too, unveiled his most sweeping urbanist intervention after a massive crisis of land usage following the Great Depression and its accompanying dispossessions. With Broadacre, Wright envisioned an intermingling of residential, urban, and green space that disrupted the dichotomy between

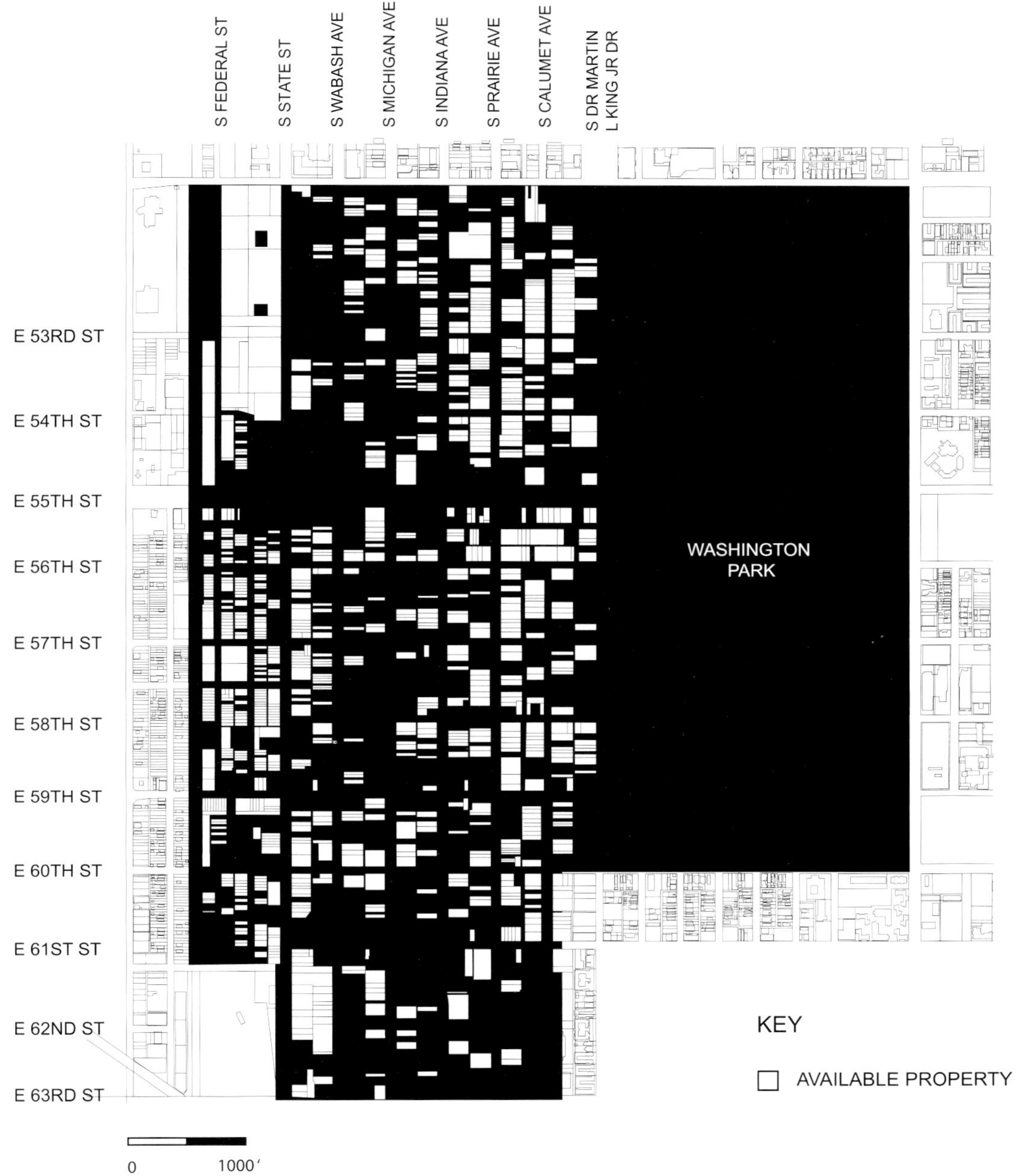

Fig. 77: Brown asserts throughout this project that land is a valuable asset. This map displays every available property in Washington Park in white, representing over 6 million square feet (151 acres), which is 35 percent of the neighborhood's developable land and an area more than half the size of the existing park. Opportunity Map, Smooth Growth, 2012. Digital map.

city and suburb, residential and agricultural. Wright's claim that in Broadacre "all is symmetrical, but it is seldom obviously and never academically so," carries forward to the studied bundles anchoring Brown's approach to Washington Park.[7]

But while Wright imagined a low-density city rippling through the landscape so as to be responsive to the specific needs of the individual citizen, the new country Freeman via Brown dreams up retains the ethos of a flowing and reactive city accommodating spectrums and differing intensities of use in the service of collective stewardship managed by groups of tenants and owners. [Fig. 76] Broadacre embodies Wright's commitment to what he deemed "the freedom to decentralize," enabling each individual to claim "his social right to his place on the ground."[8] But Brown's plan, as articulated by his fictional urbanist Freeman, whose alternative genealogy of freedom is embedded in both his name and his history, insists that one's social right to the ground is contingent on the communal management of this resource always being shaped and reshaped by the social. The social right to place is exactly that in Smooth Growth—social, navigated by collectives acting as stewards of shared space beyond the singular individual acre. [Fig. 77] While Wright designed Broadacre in reaction against the modernist city, the Washington Park envisioned in Smooth Growth is designed to facilitate care for the

city and its inhabitants in the metropolis that remains in the wake of both demographic and ecological turmoil.

But in addition to knowing the pain of disinvestment and the history of urbanism, Daniel Freeman would have grown up around the Washington Park Camera Club, the oldest predominately African American organization in the Chicago area invested in making photographs of and with their neighborhood. He would have witnessed, and maybe even marched in, the annual Bud Billiken parade, the largest African American parade in the country, which ends each year in Washington Park. And while Wright's Broadacre centered the growing dominance of the automobile, Washington Park is home to the first and oldest station within Chicago's L transit system originally designed to service visitors to the 1893 World's Columbian Exposition. With this firsthand education in composition, flow, and movement via Washington Park's own "inner rhythms," to again cite Wright, alongside his formal study of urbanist schemes past, present, and future, Freeman both draws from and upends the historical longing to reinvent the perfect American settlement. The creation of this New Country—as well as Freeman himself, who exists as an urbanist collage of sorts—comes from studiously learning from the real and imagined countries, territories, imaginaries,

Fig. 78, opposite: Marshall Brown poses as Daniel Freeman, his fictional architect from Washington Park. The photo was originally taken in Brown's studio during his residency at MacDowell in 2010. Still from *The New Country*, 2019. Looped digital animation, 00:04:38.

collectives, patterns, and settlements of old to find a new kind of texture, pace, and organizing schema for urban life. [Fig. 78]

As Brown writes in a poetic treatise capturing the epic nature of Freeman's neofrontier vision, "So-called *nature* / neither conquered / nor destroyed. Freeman's insurgent movement / filled the vacuum. A new way / Smooth Growth."[9] Refusing stark distinctions between not only urban and suburban but also private and public, abandoned and occupied, containment and the unrestrained, Brown's plan envisions growth not through massive increases in footprint, infrastructure, or population but by learning to navigate in, through, and around our infrastructural and conceptual binaries, assembling new countries from the remnants of the old.

NOTES

1   Freeman's name is an intentional nod to the protagonist of Sam Greenlee's 1969 novel, *The Spook Who Sat by the Door*, who begins the novel as the CIA's first African American agent but ends it as a freedom fighter training Chicago street gangs in guerrilla warfare to take down the government. Daniel Freeman is also the name of the first man to claim land under the Homestead Act of 1862, signing for his parcel of land in Beatrice, Nebraska, in the early hours of January 1, 1863. The Daniel Freeman that Brown conjures resonates with both of these mythoi in his various identities as strategist, survivalist, rebel, and frontiersman in addition to urbanist.

2   US Department of Commerce, *1970 Census of Population and Housing: Census Tracts, Chicago ILL., Standard Metropolitan Statistical Area, Part 1,* (Washington, DC: Bureau of the Census, 1971–72), 43–44; Chicago Metropolitan Agency for Planning, *Community Data Snapshot, Washington Park, Chicago Community Area* (June 2020), https://www.cmap.illinois. gov/documents/10180/126764/Washington+Park.pdf.

3   The bombed home occupied in real life by the young Lorraine Hansberry that inspired her canonical play, despite being in a subdivision named for Washington Park, is technically in Woodlawn just to the South. See Hansberry, *A Raisin in the Sun* (New York: Random House, 1959).

4   Olmsted and Vaux's 1868 plans for another space—the planned community of Riverside, Illinois—would incidentally serve as an influence for Smooth Growth, particularly Olmsted's determined rebellion from the Jeffersonian grid as well as his attention to the transitional spaces between public and private land in the Riverside plan.

5   See Brian McCammack, *Landscapes of Hope: Nature and the Great Migration in Chicago* (Cambridge, MA: Harvard University Press, 2017).

6   See D. Bradford Hunt, "What Went Wrong with Public Housing in Chicago? A History of the Robert Taylor Homes," *Journal of the Illinois State Historical Society* 94, no. 1 (2001): 96–123.

7   Frank Lloyd Wright, "Broadacre: A New Community Plan," *Architectural Record* 77 (1935): 244.

8   Wright, 244, 245.

9   Marshall Brown, "The New Country," *Manifest: A Journal of the Americas* 3 (2021): 265

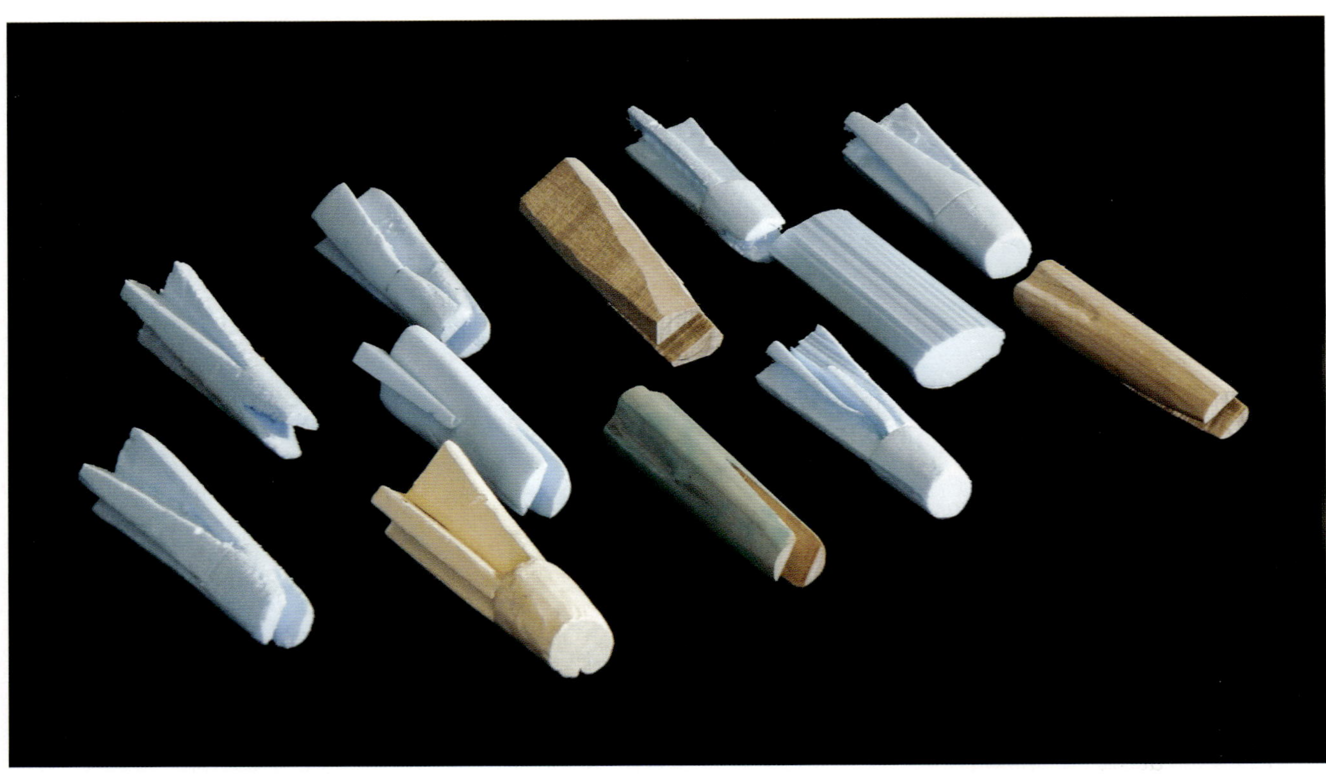

Fig. 79: Out of many, one: the search
for DCA'S monumental "cloven"
columns. These exploratory models led
to the final prototype, which is split
at the base, allowing people to walk
through with a sense of ceremonial
passage. Column Studies, Dequindre
Civic Academy, 2016. Foam, wood, and
Plastalina clay, scale: 1" = 8'-0".

Joseph Becker is a curator, writer, and educator in San Francisco. He is the Associate Curator of Architecture and Design at the San Francisco Museum of Modern Art, where he focuses on creating access points to tools, ideas, and issues surrounding the intersection of design and art, and the shifts between conceptual, experimental, and production practice.

Adrienne Brown is associate professor of English at the University of Chicago. She specializes in American and African American cultural production in the twentieth century, with an emphasis on the history of perception as shaped by the built environment. Her books include *The Black Skyscraper: Architecture and the Perception of Race* (2017) and the coedited volume *Race and Real Estate* (2015).

Marshall Brown is an architect, artist, and scholar, and associate professor at Princeton University School of Architecture. He has represented the United States at the Venice Architecture Biennale, and his work has been collected by the Art Institute of Chicago, San Francisco Museum of Modern Art, Museum of Contemporary Photography, and Crystal Bridges Museum of American Art.

Allison Glenn is senior curator and director of public art at the Contemporary Arts Museum Houston. She curated *Promise, Witness, Remembrance* (Speed Art Museum, 2021), an exhibition developed around the portrait of Breonna Taylor, painted by Amy Sherald. Formerly, Glenn was associate curator, Contemporary Art at Crystal Bridges Museum of American Art and manager of publications and curatorial associate for *Prospect.4*, the fourth edition of New Orleans's international art triennial.

Karen Kice is a consultant and curator in art, architecture, and design. Her exhibitions include *Sahara: Acts of Memory* (Benton Museum of Art at Pomona College, 2021), *Recurrent Visions: The Architecture of Marshall Brown Projects* (Princeton University School of Architecture, 2019), and *Chatter: Architecture Talks Back* (Art Institute of Chicago, 2015). For five years, she was a curator in the Department of Architecture and Design at the Art Institute of Chicago.

Mónica Ponce de León is a professor and dean of the School of Architecture at Princeton University and founding principal of MPdL Studio. From 2008 through 2015, she was the dean of Taubman College at the University of Michigan. For over twelve years, Ponce de León taught at the Graduate School of Design at Harvard, where she became a professor and served as the Graduate Program coordinator and director of the Digital Fabrication Lab.

Acknowledgments

—

I am grateful, first, to my family. Yvonne and Mia provide the love and encouragement that sustains me every day. My parents, Harold and Verniece, provided me with the foundation and confidence to pursue my dreams.

Thanks always to the City of Chicago. Donna Robertson hired me to teach at IIT in 2008, was tremendously supportive, and provided impeccable advice when needed along the way. When I first arrived, Stephanie Smith was my chaperone, introduced me to everyone, and became my collaborator and dear friend. Leroy Kennedy helped me navigate Chicago's South Side. Allison Davis and Jared Davis sheltered my practice at the Overton Hygienic Building for seven years, making much of the work presented here possible. Ghian Foreman first welcomed me to Washington Park. Brandon Johnson commissioned the first Smooth Growth master plan, which was later funded by the Graham Foundation for the Arts. Scott Speh at Western Exhibitions reminded me that architecture is also art and helped my work reach new audiences. Lynn Hauser and Neil Ross became my role models for friendship, generosity, and joie de vivre. Geof Oppenheimer provided comradery, constant debate, and critical advice about exhibitions. Conor O'Neil shared his passions for adventure and generosity. Kim Soss at the IIT College of Architecture welcomed me during my first days in Crown Hall and provided invaluable support of many kinds. Amanda Williams brought the gifts of solidarity, humor, and color.

Many thanks to my colleagues everywhere. Mónica Ponce de León provided critical support for this book, which began as an exhibition at Princeton University School of Architecture. Laura Miller and Richard Sommer taught, endured, mentored, and encouraged me for more than twenty years. Jay Chatterjee was the first to teach me about academic life and has remained an essential sounding board. The Honorable Letitia James showed tremendous confidence in me from the very beginning.

Thank you to everyone who worked to make this, my first book, a reality. Jennifer Thompson and Princeton Architectural Press believed in this project from the beginning. Karen Kice worked tirelessly on this publication—I am fortunate to have such a friend and collaborator. Joseph Becker, Adrienne Brown, and Allison Glenn brought insightful reflections to this volume, and each of them has supported my work in various ways.

And finally, thank you, Architecture, for the intellectual pleasures and creative struggles that have shaped my understanding of the world.

—Marshall Brown

The following individuals contributed to the following projects:

For the Yards Development Workshop, John Nafziger and Sarah Strauss were my initial partners. Anna Dietzsch and Alex Felson collaborated on the design for the UNITY Plan, and Ron Shiffman and Tom Angotti provided mentorship and material support.

For the Dequindre Civic Academy, Allison Cottle and Sudeshna Sen worked as design assistants.

For Smooth Growth Urbanism®, Sarah Hanson Salgado assisted with the design and developed the landscape strategy. Nadia Shah researched and developed the cost analysis. Hyesun Jeong, Jake Emery, Kareem Cousar, Marina Mazagatos, and Sonya Shah assisted with site analysis and modeling.

My gratitude for this project extends from my time
in Chicago, where I first met Marshall Brown. I think
fondly of his warm welcome, which provided
a strong foundation for our friendship and collabora-
tions to flourish. I am grateful for the opportunities
Marshall has provided for us to collaborate, where
I got to know his work more intimately and develop
a deeper understanding of him. Through his work,
he has given me a new perspective of architecture
and urbanism.

Thank you, always, to my family for their love and
support, which has created a vital foundation to
explore my passions.

I share gratitude with Marshall to Mónica Ponce
de León and Princeton University School of
Architecture for their support, and to the contributors
who helped shape this publication.

—Karen Kice

This publication is made possible in
part by the Barr Ferree Foundation Fund
for Publications, Department of Art
and Archaeology, Princeton University.

Published by
Princeton Architectural Press
70 West 36th Street
New York, NY 10018
www.papress.com

ISBN 978-1-64896-068-0

Production Editor: Kristen Hewitt
Designers: Paul Wagner, Natalie Snodgrass

Library of Congress Control Number: 2021949637

Image credits
—
All images in this publication, unless otherwise
noted, are courtesy of Marshall Brown Projects.
Fig. 4 © Museo Nacional del Prado
Fig. 6 Photograph by Marshall Brown
Fig. 10 © Wayne Andrews/Esto
Fig. 16 New York State GIS
Fig. 23 Photograph by Marshall Brown
Fig. 24 © Jonathan Barkey, 2006
Fig. 27 Courtesy of Michael Sorkin Studio
Fig. 28 Photograph by Marshall Brown
Fig. 46 © The Federal State Budget Institution of
    Culture Shchusev State Museum of Architecture
Fig. 47 The Noguchi Museum Archives, 151423.
    © INFGM / ARS
Fig. 50 Photograph by Marshall Brown
Fig. 74 Image from GIS Illinois
Fig. 75 © Camilo José Vergara
Fig. 76 FGP / Archive Photos via Getty Images
Endpapers: © Michelle Litvin Studio